Stoic Philosophy Bundle

Stoic Philosophy Bundle

(Books 1 and 2)

Featuring Stoicism – Understanding and Practicing the Philosophy of the Stoics

&

Stoicism – Purpose and Perspectives

Kyle Faber

Stoic Philosophy Bundle (Books 1 and 2)

Published by CAC Publishing LLC
ISBN: 978-1-950010-43-1 paperback
ISBN: 978-1-950010-42-4 eBook

Table of Contents

Stoicism

Understanding and Practicing the Philosophy of the Stoics

Stoicism

Understanding and Practicing the Philosophy of the Stoics

Your Guide to Wisdom, Freedom,

Happiness, and Living the Good Life

Kyle Faber

Stoicism – Understanding and Practicing the Philosophy of the Stoics

Published by CAC Publishing LLC
ISBN: 978-1-950010-25-7 paperback
ISBN: 978-1-950010-24-0 eBook

This book is dedicated to those that truly wish to live the good life. Stoicism is not about money or fancy things, it's about living your best life regardless of what's around you. To escape the daily pressures and bland existence we trap ourselves in.

Introduction

"Only the educated are free."

— **Epictetus**

Stoicism is a deep and penetrating topic that does not lend itself to rapid instruction and shallow practice. Its nuances and complexities are best absorbed gradually and with deliberate attention paid to the details. Understanding Stoicism can't be done at arm's length by instruction alone. It requires a two-way connection between the teacher and the student. The teacher lays out the philosophy in gradual steps, and the student absorbs it, reflects on it, practices it, and then builds on it before putting it all together in his or her own mind.

It is nothing like a recipe where one starts with the ingredients, follows the steps, and places it in the oven and voilà a cake appears. Stoicism is not dessert. It is a philosophy, and it is also a way of life that comes from an internal fountain and is in harmony with external forces. For something to be a way of life, you have to live it, and you have to experiment with it and adapt it to your personal situation.

If you are expecting a book that is going to be a step-by-step how-to book that will somehow miraculously transform your state of mind to a Stoic's state of existence, then you will face disappointment early. You should, instead, be prepared to go much deeper, treading slowly, pausing at each incremental stage to acclimate yourself.

The goal of this book is to reveal the soul of the Stoic and methods by which that soul forms so that one may chart a path toward that outcome. The book does not presume any prior knowledge of Stoicism. Come as you are. It is what it is, and so whether you are a student of Greek philosophy or a total novice interested in bringing peace into your life, this book places you on the path you need to make it so.

The two intellectual giants of Western civilization—the Greeks and the Romans— provided the reservoir of observations, advice, and understanding of the human soul, the nature of the universe, and how the two collide. It is embodied in the sea of work that resulted in such philosophies as Stoicism. The pursuit of Stoic philosophy today is just as relevant as it was back then simply because we are all searching for the truth, and the best way to ascertain that truth is to be able to develop a framework in which to observe it, practice it, and internalize it.

Chapter 1 - Framework of Stoic Philosophy

"Everything we hear is an opinion, not a fact. Everything we see is a perspective, not the truth."

— Emperor Marcus Aurelius Antoninus Augustus, 180 AD

Around 300 BC, just after the death of Alexander the Great, the intellectual influence that straddled the region stretching from the Mediterranean to the foot of the Himalayan range was propelled by the momentum that came with the Hellenistic conquest of the region.

From the farthest extent of Aryan lands in northern India to the architectural wonders of Babylon in West Asia, Alexander had spread an intellectual curiosity that gave rise to the amalgamation and acceptance of Western philosophies that eventually resulted in the amalgamation and proliferation of Western civilization.

As the Hellenistic age prepared to advance and breathe life into the Roman Republic and then into Imperial Rome, a new breed of thinkers emerged and brought with them the foundations of an old philosophy to take on new roots. They started to identify and answer questions surrounding life living, and through dialectic processes formulated a series of philosophical guardrails, grammatical rules, and ideological tenets that formed the framework of a key school of thought that would go on to become the basis of the grammar we use in communication today, the process of inquiry that is the basis to develop science and technologies, and also as the basis of major religions.

To be clear, this was not just the work of one man but rather a collaborative effort that started at the steps of the Agora in post-Socratic times (some will argue, earlier) and developed all the way to Emperor Marcus Aurelius' palace in Rome. Much of the philosophy that resulted was rooted in the arguments and ideas that transpired among men of crystal-clear thought and rock-solid virtue. They attempted to distill from collaborative life lessons a body of knowledge that would clearly and succinctly become the keys to inner peace and wisdom and the means by which they could conquer it.

What resulted from this intellectual cauldron was a set of virtues unheard of until that time and which came to be known as Stoicism. Those who practiced it came to famously be known as Stoics.

In ancient Greece, the word "Stoic" didn't exist as any verb or noun. The leading philosophies and schools of thought of the day were named according to the place in which the teachers of that philosophy gathered to exchange ideas and information. So, if today, you got together at your local library's porch to discuss your particular philosophy, it would come to be known as the "Porch Philosophy." In the same way, the thinkers of the intellectual philosophy used to congregate at the portico at the Agora in Athens, and so it came to be known as the philosophy of the painted portico. In Greek, that is called *"Stoa Poikile."* You can see how that gradually morphed into Stoic and on to Stoicism.

Stoic represents the person, while Stoa or Stoicism represents the philosophy.

The intellectual giants of the period, including Socrates; his students Plato, Euclid, and Xenophon; and their students, such as Aristotle, discussed various ideas over the course of a century, from the time of Socrates, circa 400 BC, to the time of Zeno's founding of Stoicism in 301 BC, a century of debate and reflection by men of towering intellect distilling what we now regard as this philosophy of the Stoics.

If nothing else, it should tell you that the philosophy we are looking at is something that has been synthesized and distilled by some of the most intellectual minds of the classical era over a significant period of time. It is a decidedly cerebral and sober observation of the nature of all things and the harmonious course of action, which is easily adaptable to today's world.

As Greek dominance gave way to Roman hegemony and Roman influence spread to the provinces, the philosophical center of gravity shifted to the amphitheaters in Rome. Here, the likes of Seneca the Younger and the sixteenth emperor of the Roman Empire, Marcus Aurelius, adopted the philosophy and propelled it forward, allowing it to gain traction and mainstream attention.

If you were thinking that Stoicism began in Rome, just know that that is a common fallacy. It actually started in Greece and moved to Rome over time to become the mores of the educated, not the religion of the masses.

Early Religions

While Stoicism is not a religion, comparing it to religions prevalent in those times has its advantages and its limits. Philosophers taught students how to think, not what to think. In essence, philosophy paved the way for the student to discover the truth. Religion does the same thing but goes one step further. It allows the human mind to project outward to a higher being, and that being becomes the personification of all things that the human mind cannot comprehend or undertake. It served a powerful purpose. It became the catchall of all unknowns.

For instance, in the days of early marine endeavors, as the Greeks boarded their triremes for war on distant shores, they had no concept of weather, climate, tide, and wind. They could not predict what the elements would do once the fleet set sail. They didn't know about weather fronts moving over the area or about pressure systems causing heavy rain or strong winds. They didn't understand the basic mechanics of wind and tide above what they could easily observe. They left what they didn't know to the whims of the gods. In other words, what the human mind could not comprehend but still observe, it ascribed to one almighty hidden force. To conform to the human mind, they personified that force and called it God.

From there, the God of Sea, the God of War, the God of the Sun, and others were brought forth. Those deities formed the early multigod universe, which then evolved into a unitary and almighty god universe that was adopted by the new religion of Christianity that took hold during the time of Emperor Constantine.

Many wars also resulted from religious roots, which can be taken as further proof that religion serves as the wild card—whenever we don't understand something, including our emotional hostility, political hostility, and seeming differences—we assign and ascribe it to religion, just as the Greek sailors ascribed climatology to invisible gods.

Religions back then were divided across two camps: ones that symbolized and were personified by deities—the manifestation of the mind's observation and the desire to worship what humans thought were the powers that ruled over them. Worship was both an attempt to pay adulation to the gods to curry favor and also to ask for things they wanted that seemed beyond their own grasp.

The second kind of religion involved nature. Naturalists and pagan worshipers reflected the thought of the power of nature over humans. As the church took hold in later centuries, it became outlawed and looked down upon. Many of these practitioners of nature worship were labeled as heretics and witches and eventually killed at the stake.

By the time the Greeks had brought religion into the mainstream, they were also pursuing intellectual paths that were the product of rational thought. It seemed then and still does now that religion and rational thought occupied opposite ends of nature's spectrum.

To get a wide-ranging picture, it is also wise to touch briefly on the issue of spirituality, which is not the same as theology, and those who are agnostic or atheists by choice would typically tend to gravitate toward spirituality at some point and find that it has more to offer than the theology of organized religions.

That is to be expected, and you can visualize this with something more common. Think about food. Think about how food is prepared when it is done by a chef for just a small family. Consider the amount of time and care that goes into the preparation and the level of individualization that it can afford. On the other hand, if you were buying pre-prepared, mass-produced food, what you would get is something highly mechanized, highly processed, and significantly less nutritious. Philosophies are the same way. When you take time and focus on something in philosophy and religion and do it over a long period of time, you find that it takes on an organic flavor. However, when you mass-produce a religion, it has a more processed flavor and ends up leaving a bad taste in your mouth.

One way to approach this tapestry is to see that spirituality is not as heavy on dogma as religion is; religion is not as heavy on logic and reasoning as philosophy is, and philosophy is not as ethereal as spirituality. When you see it this way, what you will also see if you pull your focus back is that they are all part of a seamless tapestry that exists in three dimensions.

This book is concerned only with the philosophical aspect of this tapestry, and more specifically it is only focusing on the philosophy of the Stoics. Numerous other philosophies exist, and all of them have something to offer their students. As you will see in the chapter on historical roots, many of these philosophies find their genesis in the logic and thinking of Socrates a hundred years before. You will also see that we all exist on a spectrum. Nothing is distinctly different from something else, for example, Stoics have similarities to Cynics, who have similarities to Epicureans, who have similarities to academicians.

The religion, culture, and thinking of Greece evolved and was transplanted during the inception of Rome by Romulus and Remus. In its early days, Greece was a loose construct of city-states stretching from the Aegean Sea to the eastern shores of the Mediterranean. One of the largest of these cities was Troy. Upon the siege of Troy and its eventual sacking and razing, the inhabitants who survived, however few, left the burning city and made their way on foot to Italy. One of these people was a man by the name of Aeneas. Under his leadership, the former citizens of Troy set up a new village. In short order, the descendants of this village were transplanted to another city that was created on the slopes of Mount Alba, which they named

Alba Longa. This city is where Romulus and Remus, founders of Rome, were born.

The teachings, philosophy, religions, culture, and technology made a clear and direct path from the fragmented city-states of Greece into the fabric of Rome from the very first moment of its birth.

The religion and academics of Greece were part of the soul of Rome. While the teachings in Rome evolved as the city was gradually being built and maturing, parallels in their thinking evolved as well. The elites in Rome not only learned to read and speak Latin but were also inclined to study Greek so that they could tap into the intellectual veins of resources rooted in Athens in particular and Greece as a whole in general.

Men like Julius Caesar and some of the emperors after him were schooled in Greek literature and philosophy, and that formed the intellectual basis of the Roman mind-set. At the same time, the Roman age and the expansion of the empire allowed the proliferation of ideas and ideals across the provinces.

As religions took hold, it was a form of hope that spread across the masses like wildfire. It was a psychological panacea to almost any difficulty that was prevalent, and it allowed the citizens of Greece and Rome to postpone today's pain in hopes of tomorrow's potential. That was the key to every religion. Whether it was the desire for revenge or good fortune or even the need for a larger-than-life protector for whatever seemed like a larger-than-life threat, religion gave the ancient masses access to an all-powerful being that could make it happen.

From the perspective of theological history, religions served a particular purpose to alleviate pain and give hope. This theology was hijacked and weaponized by politics and politicians. When Rome was on the cusp of imperialism and Caesar had just been murdered by those close to him, it happened to be a time when Hailey's Comet was coming into view. It proved to be the perfect time for Caesar's nephew and adopted heir, Octavius, to point to the sky and tell the world that what they saw in the sky was his uncle rising to heaven to take his seat as a god.

The trickery worked. The public believed it, and they started to see Julius as a deity and Octavian, who later renamed himself Augustus, as the son of a god. It was a brilliant political ploy that worked. The people of Rome then went on to beg and force Augustus to become emperor. He actually never asked for the job, and, in fact, he shunned it at first, which made them want him to be emperor even more. Augustus gave the masses hope as the son of god and became the earthly nexus to heavenly power. Not too far from where that was happening a young boy was born, who grew up to become a carpenter, and was claiming the same thing.

We see across civilizations and time that the need for a superhuman being manifests in many ways, and some grow popular enough to become a religion. There is definitely a place for religious dogma and teachings in the tapestry of the human condition. It is a small part of understanding a complex and multidimensional universe, but it isn't the be all and end all that it is sometimes considered to be. As mentioned earlier in the book, there is a three-dimensional tapestry of truth that is stretched across religion, philosophy, and spirituality. Without truly understanding religion, however foreign it may be to our own mind-set, we are robbed of the diversity of thought that eventually assists in the understanding of truth.

Understanding it is as important to the future development of the mind as the development of internal peace that one feels when knowing that they have something greater than themselves to handle difficulties that can seem greater than their individual might.

Stoicism addresses this tapestry perfectly because it has hidden religious and spiritual aspects that make it one of the most comprehensive philosophies that give you a better picture of the truth. It also ends up giving you a better framework to develop the ability to experience the truth within yourself. In other words, Stoicism straddles the center of balance in the philosophical, religious, and spiritual tapestry.

Not all Stoicism is about religion or spirituality, but it has features of Christianity, Deism, Buddhism, and other major religions. It may be hard for those of you who are agnostic or atheistic to even consider the notion that such similarities exist with organized religion and the philosophy of Stoicism. Stoic philosophy does not discount the existence of an all-powerful force of creation. In essence, this force is monolithic and unitary in the same way that Christianity is monotheistic and suggests an omnipotent and omnipresent god.

Stoicism is constantly asking a larger question, which is more than just about being stoic or pensive in nature. The larger question that Stoics and Christians ask is related to the purpose of one's life.

Stoics are constantly attempting to delve deeper into the root of existence and the need to make that existence worthwhile. It turns out that just as Socrates and Heraclitus had suspected and observed a life that is spent in pursuit of a greater purpose is one that works out better. In Christianity, the purpose of life has been to serve God, and a life that is devoted to that purpose is one that was considered blessed.

Like similarities between Stoicism and Christianity, there are also similarities between Stoic observations and Buddhist teachings. Although they both evolved two hundred years apart, one in the Mediterranean and the other at the foot of the Himalayas, they both seem to follow very similar trains of thought.

On the one hand, Stoics consider that happiness is found within one's self and not susceptible or manipulated by factors external to the soul, and Buddhists believe that peace can only come from within if it is to have any value. Their similarities in this basic tenet are striking in the fact that only things that are universally true could be developed independently with the same result.

In Buddhism, the path to Nirvana (enlightenment, for lack of a better word) is to follow a prescribed path. This path encapsulates a set of actions, perception frameworks, and thought processes that one can develop over the course of life to acquire an enlightened state. This path includes the practice of cultivating the right perspective, having the right aspiration, invoking proper speech patterns, engaging in appropriate actions (and disengaging from inappropriate ones), embracing proper living, cultivating deep concentration, and invoking perpetual mindfulness.

If you already have a background in Stoic philosophy, you will realize that most of the elements along this path sound familiar. In Stoic philosophy, the main root that is identical to Buddhism is that the individual is responsible for his own happiness (and, conversely, his own suffering) and, as such, he or she is responsible for the consequences that plague him or her down the road. In other words, if you choose to be happy, you need only to look inside yourself to actions that will consequently lead to the state of happiness you desire. Those consequences are the sum of a number of factors not limited to just the person's actions but also reflective of their perspective and perception, their goals and aspirations, their conversations, righteous living, focus, reflection, and meditation.

The other thing that is almost identical but differs slightly from the Christian-Stoic similarities is that Buddhism does not compel anyone to worship anyone or anything. Followers of the Buddhist way use the statue of Siddhartha Gautama (widely known as Buddha) to remind them of the embodiment of his principles, while Stoics do not necessarily have a personification of their tenets of Stoicism. Many Stoics display busts or portraits of Stoic philosophers in their personal space to remind them of their principles, but those artifacts are not used to worship—only to remind.

That doesn't mean you couldn't have a symbolic reminder of Stoic teachings. A model of the Parthenon is just as good, or the image of Marcus Aurelius would serve the purpose as long as you realize that you are not paying homage to the picture, the bust, or the person. It is merely a way to represent the ideals of the philosophy. Remember the old adage that a picture is worth a thousand words. That's what the picture or statue of Buddha or Marcus Aurelius is supposed to do for you. In one glance, it is designed to bring all the associative thoughts of the principles that bring you happiness and clarity.

The next similarity that plays between the two philosophies is the definition of happiness. Stoicism talks about happiness in almost the same way as Buddhism, and they have similar definitions of happiness as well. That is the key before any further discussion in Stoicism because happiness that is derived from external sources remains at the whim of that source. As such, material happiness comes inherently with self-destruction. The most beautiful flower will wilt, money will erode, palaces will crumble, and gold can one day become worthless. Buddhism and Stoicism do not consider happiness as something that comes from money and possessions but rather as a state that manifests in the wake of practicing and understanding wisdom, courage, and justice. In this respect, happiness in Christianity has a similar meaning. In the Bible, it is said that a rich man entering heaven is like a camel entering the eye of a needle, which is impossible. If you think that heaven is a point in space and a place you go to, then this makes little sense, but if you equate, for academic purposes, that heaven, Nirvana, and enlightenment are the same thing, then you start to see that happiness is a state, and you cannot enter that state while you are distracted by the pitfalls of wealth, the longing for wealth, the disappointment of not obtaining that wealth, or dealing with the consequences of trying to attain wealth immorally.

The next aspect of similarity between Buddhists and Stoics is that they are encouraged to be part of a collective and to contribute to that collective. Whether that collective means you take on some form of public service, whether you take on family responsibilities, or you look after your neighbors doesn't matter, but the essence of the two philosophies promotes the idea of unitary strength. In Stoicism, it is embodied in their propensity to duty.

In the current state of world affairs, happiness has been hijacked, or rather, the definition of happiness has been hijacked in a way that is prevalent and pervasive. We see the idea of happiness limited to the fleeting nature of consumerism and the physical feeling of bliss. There is really nothing wrong with that concept. It is perfectly acceptable for a person to feed the desires of feeling. After all, they are already within us. The confusion and the long-term definition according to Stoicism is that it can get to the point of being a considerable distraction to the efforts and actions that one needs to take to reach that level of peace and happiness.

Departure from Religion

The problem with the typical person's understanding of religion whether they were taught this way or if they were naturally of that mind-set comes from the fact that they were given a set of rules and told to practice it. That leads to all action and no spirit. They go through the motions, doing the rituals without ever understanding what they are doing and what that symbolizes.

Catholics are told to go to church on Sunday, abstain during Lent, go for confession, and receive Holy Communion. Each action and ritual has a purpose designed to evoke a certain internal manifestation. As St. Thomas Aquinas, a philosopher and devout Catholic, articulated in his writings about rituals and inner spirit, external actions are an "outward action of an inward grace."

Religions weave rituals into their practice as a way to evoke manifestations of spirituality from within so that they can come into contact with a higher power. If those actions are just meant to be limited to just the action, however, then that desired spirituality is left out in the cold.

Followers of religions, during prayer, be it Catholics at mass, Hindus at puja, or Muslims at maghrib, are reaching toward a higher purpose. Most do as they have been told and follow the dogma and the rituals without ever understanding the true nature of their actions or where it came from. In time, the spirit of the ritual was forgotten, and only the vacant actions remained, leaving the congregant vacant inside without fulfillment and eventually void of happiness.

The original intent of the teachings in these religions, be it Islam, Christianity, or Hinduism, was to evoke a sense of spirituality, but over time that intent has been lost. If you look carefully at the original words of the founders of the religions or the ancient texts that these religions rest on, you will find that much of what was actually prescribed then is lost today.

With deeper analysis, though, you can see that what they tried to explain does seem to show up in Stoic philosophy, especially when referring to happiness. In Buddhism, they don't look at it in terms of happiness as much as they try to prevent suffering, and they do that by altering their desires and perception just as the Stoics prescribe. In Christianity, they focus on sins of excess, such as gluttony, lust, and greed, and you find that Stoicism as well talks about the pursuit of happiness, which is not found in any of those excesses. Epictetus writes that freedom is not attained by procuring that which is desired but from controlling the desire.

With that in mind, it is also not accurate or equitable to blame the evolution of religion into a vacant set of practices and rituals. A true understanding of theology and spirituality requires time, and most people do not have much of that following a particular lifestyle. They had also lost the plot in most cases not because they were ignorant but rather because they were walking into the proverbial theater in the middle of the third act. The premise of religion failed to pass the intellectual test or the test of logic that a more evolved mind today seeks to understand.

What was missing was any real intellectual philosophy that jived with the logic and reasoning that such people as Socrates and his students had advocated two thousand years ago. Most of the religions and teachings back then did not comport with the powers of reasoning and dialectic debate but instead scratched the surface of observation.

That brings us back to Stoicism today. To dive into Stoicism is to try to understand its intent as well as what people before you have thought and what people after you might think about it.

Rituals

Organized religion is organized because its aim is to get the message out to as many people as possible, and that requires organization. On the other hand, archaic and nonorganized religions were just observations of a higher power and the lack of the human mind to comprehend and be empowered by it. None of it was wrong. It was just who we are and what was available to us at the time.

Take, for instance, the idea of rituals. There were all kinds of rituals in the ancient world—rituals to sacrifice animals and rituals to sacrifice humans—rituals to offer alcohol and rituals to offer food. Other rituals offered words of praise and adulation and burning of candles. All these rituals had a special place in the human psyche and were enhanced with the performance of the ritual that got the participant what he or she desired.

Alexander the Great, the youngest conqueror in history and who swung the Hellenistic philosophies to the east, was a great general and master tactician. But if he were to sit across from you now and you asked what he owed his success to, he would undoubtedly say that it was because of all the rituals he performed before every battle. Alexander would pour libations and offer sacrifices to the gods before every battle, and he would offer thanks at the end of each fight. He is also the only general in history to remain undefeated no matter the odds.

You may wonder whether the gods really hear you when you invoke their help or are they really swayed by your offerings. We may never know the answer to that, but we do know that rituals work, which is why they have been part of every religion in ancient times and today. Even the Catholic Church employs rituals, although they are not called as such. The Hindus in India have numerous rituals as do other lesser-known religions around the world.

We don't really know how they work, but they do. If you believe and perform the ritual, you end up getting what you ask for. In modern-day metaphysics, it is part of the Law of Attraction. Stoics place gravity on rituals, but they do not do so blindly or without the intellectual component attached. They are mindful of the rituals and do not stop at what they know but rather seek greater depth in their practice and their understanding. How does this concern us today in our discussion of Stoicism? It is because rituals have worked since long ago, and we see what works, so we keep doing it. We observed and then we repeated. It also concerns us today because Stoics perform rituals of wisdom. Observation and cogitation became rituals.

Observation

Stoic philosophy has two sides regarding this same effect—observing and then doing. The first is that Stoicism takes observation to a much deeper level. In the early days, Stoics sitting around the Agora used their senses to observe and then brought their observations to a debate and created frameworks to make other hypotheses. Stoicism was, in part, a sort of the derivative and higher level of observation. If you observed the world of rituals, that would be simple observations. It is like having a lucky sock. If you realize that each time you wear that sock you win the game, then you will start wearing that sock every time you play the game. The moment you wore that sock it placed you in a mind-set that caused you to perform better, and what you observed was just really the superficial layer of it.

Stoicism, however, didn't just look at the luck of the sock. It went one step further and started to think about what would connect the dots between the act of wearing that sock and winning the game.

The other side of the coin was logic, which was undoubtedly the vestiges of Socratic teachings. Logic has a bad reputation today. We tend to take the Captain Kirk point of view of this instead of Dr. Spock's. (By the way, Spock was modeled after the quintessential Stoic.)

Some of us think that logic is too dry and not how life was created or how it progresses today, but you may have a wrong and simplistic view of what reasoning and logic are and what they bring to the table when learning about the higher power of the human condition.

We are the leading edge—the latest iteration of billions of years of evolution. (I did say billions because I don't consider the evolution of man to be just over the span of time ranging from the first trilobites; let's consider the evolution of man since the Big Bang). You can't look at life as just the moment when plants and animals came into being for this discussion. That would be incomplete, and that is mostly the reason why it is impossible for non-Stoics to see that we are all part of the same universe.

Stoics see two parts to this equation of life. You can think of all things in this universe as animate or inanimate objects. This is what the Stoics began to understand all those centuries ago. They may not have had insight into the microscopic elements of the human body, but they had reasoned out the nature of living, the elements of life, and the change that is part of everything.

Change according to Stoics is the only constant, and it is that change that you consider to be life. Change signifies and encapsulated the existence of life. Without change, there can be no life.

Even the erosion of solid rock by a stream is an indication of life and nature. It is not the water that erodes the mighty rock but rather the movement. Just as we can see that is not the water that causes the erosion but the movement of water (the element of change), you must also apply the same element of change to see that life exists from that.

The point here is that Stoics distinguish the tangible from the intangible. Tangible covers all the things that you can describe and discern directly from your senses. For example, if you can see it, hold it, touch it, and taste it, that means it is tangible. In fact, if you can ascribe a characteristic to it, that makes it tangible. But these tangible phenomena do not exist in a vacuum. Something holds them together, and that is what we think about as the intangible.

Take, for instance, a car that is stationary. The tangible is the car; on the other hand, the intangible (and this is hard to see at first) is the fact that it is stationary. When the car is moving, however, the tangible is still the car, but the intangible now is its motion. Your eyes do not see movement. You only think they do. It is your mind that "sees" the motion. How does it do that? How does your mind "see" motion?

Your mind sees one picture frame and then compares it to the previous frame. If there is a change in the content, then it detects there is movement. It's like comparing two still shots of a moving car. On one you see the car on the left of the image, and in the second you see it in the center. Your mind then computes the difference, and you realize that the car is in motion. In the days before digital cameras, you needed video to capture frames of images, and then when it is played, the mind sees the illusion of movement.

In the physical world, your eyes see the tangible, but you need your mind to detect the intangible. If you just see the tangible in frames and do not have the mind to discern the intangible, you will be at a disadvantage as to the understanding of all things and their nature. This phenomenon of understanding and of knowledge then develops into the intractable problem in epistemology.

The reason many things in this universe—from metaphysics to spirituality—seem to be the thinking of quacks and folklore is that science demands tangible evidence so that we can all see, feel, touch, hear, and smell as evidentiary proof of a phenomenon's existence, but the most important elements of the universe are intangible.

I can share two examples to highlight this point.

The first would be the existence of something called dark matter. As recently as just two decades ago, science was committed to espousing the notion that space is a void. Scientists said that there was nothing in space, and they confirmed it by saying that it was self-evident. Because they couldn't prove the existence of interstitial matter, they said there was nothing there. We now know that to be totally false. The darkness of space is filled with what we now know to be dark matter. Just because it was not something we could detect with our five senses or any of the instruments that we built to enhance those senses we automatically thought that it wasn't there.

The second example is the existence of black holes in space. We never knew they existed, but

Albert Einstein through inspiration and calculation—and never once visiting space—determined that phenomena existed in space that later came to be known as black holes. He didn't see, touch, feel, or hear any kind of black hole, yet he knew that it would be there. Instead of seeing with his eyes, he "saw" with his mind. Truth requires appreciation by the mind and not by the senses.

The point between the two examples so far is to show that you need to use your mind to see the things that exist beyond what is merely tangible, and it is those things that are intangible that combine with the tangible to make the world what it is. Without observing the intangible, we will not be able to fully understand everything else.

To a Stoic, the philosophy that came about from all the discussions is one that attempts to continuously find the nature and character of things, which gets you closer to seeing the intangible of all things, and when you can see those intangible factors, then you can also see that all things are connected in some way at a very deep level.

As you advance through this book, the point that you should hold in the back of your mind is that the Stoics are in search of the truth. They do this in all situations and in all things, tangible and intangible, animate and inanimate. The truth they seek is not limited to something that one can see or hear, and as such you need to observe with your mind and not just your eyes.

Stoicism is not about a set of rules that get you to see the truth. They don't lead you with rules to the gates of understanding. Stoicism is not dogmatic, and neither are its benefits achieved from actions following rote memory.

It is the revelations that it makes with allegories, principles, teachings, and experiences of other practitioners that prompt you to see things in a way that makes you come to your own epiphany. Stoics are crafted from the powers of their own observation and not hammered into acquiescence from the canons of organized instructions.

It takes time to think and reflect—two essential skills that form the prerequisite of any aspirant of Stoic living and then graduate to seeing the nature of things—the inanimate we discussed earlier. There are no rules; there are only best practices and experiences of men who have climbed so high atop the pinnacle of intellectual truth that we sometimes need a sprinkle of faith to follow in their footsteps; otherwise, we will not be able to understand or see what they see.

There is one other battle that you have to wage if you are indeed interested in seeing the truth, and that is to shed the limitations of your evolved body. Many parts of you are still catching up to what you know today, but it is still part of what you were yesterday. By that, I am referring to the sense of fear that is in all man today. We fear, and thus we are unable to climb. We fear, and thus we are unable to see. We fear, and thus we are left static and immobile.

Being Stoic is by nature to be dynamic in one's understanding. You cannot be stagnant in your quest or your effort but rather to see all there is to see and yet still remain at peace and in a state of calm while pondering and executing each move deliberately and with full knowledge of what happens next. The Buddhists have a simile that describes this, and it is referred to as the Simile of the Raft.

The abridged version of this is that a man roaming the forest comes to a river that would be impossible to swim across. Seeing that he needs to cross, he decides to build a raft from the many logs, branches, and twigs, and the grass that grows on the banks. After some time and considerable effort, he completes a sturdy boat and sets sail across the river. Once he reaches the other side, he is hesitant to leave this boat on the shore and considers carrying it on his back as he proceeds on his way through the forest. On one hand, he is not willing to put in such a magnitude of effort to carry the boat on his back, but on the other hand, he does not wish to leave his hard work behind.

In the pursuit of truth, we often come across many tools that we use to help us gain momentary advantage and to cross raging waters to get to the other side. Once on the other side, we tend to do like this man did. We carry the raft on our backs for miles. At this point, the raft goes from being a tool to being a burden.

There is a process of evolution that we go through as we approach the truth. As long as we continue on this path and leave the old tools behind, we will be free to see each experience without the burden and with appropriate perspective. This is the way to see things as they are.

Chapter 2 - Historical Roots of Stoic Philosophy

"It is high time for thee, to understand that there is somewhat in thee, better and more divine than either thy passions or thy sensual appetites and affections. What is now the object of my mind, is it fear, or suspicion, or lust, or any such thing? To do nothing rashly without some certain end; let that be thy first care. The next, to have no other end than the common good. "

— Meditations, Emperor Marcus Aurelius Antoninus Augustus, 180AD

The Athenian philosopher Socrates remains the titan and anchor of modern Western thinking. His influence spread across Greece and on to the provinces of Rome and then on to the Western world, still referenced and studied intensely today.

It would take volumes to describe and explain all of his teachings and ideas, but three are relevant to the topic of Stoicism and its history. The crux of these three legs strongly advocates the need for self-understanding, and he is widely cited for saying that *"the unexamined life is not worth living."*

The first leg of his teachings strenuously advocates the fact that one needs to discover his/her own purpose and to do it on their own. Most of his teachings were based on the idea that we can find most of our answers within, and reflection and meditation provide the necessary tools to do that.

The second leg of his teachings involves the care of one's soul. In his words, the soul refers to the being beyond the flesh. It is more important than any physical component of the body, and it goes beyond the mere brain. The soul is the intangible within us that we can't see using our senses, but we can detect it if we use our mind. The care of the soul that he talks about, and it can be found in Plato's writings (since Socrates himself never wrote books or pamphlets), are ways in thought and action that do not degrade the existence. Most of this is achieved by refraining from indulgence in excess and not allowing pleasures to dictate actions.

The third and final leg of his teachings touches on the need to act out the goodness of the soul in terms of the way one interacts with others. His whole idea was not to evangelize but rather to exercise. Even in his own teachings he didn't explicitly lay out tenets and rules; instead, he employed a new way of teaching in those days, and it has come to be known as the Socratic method, and that method has become the basis of Stoic inquiry.

This method was simple to break down any observation or unknown into a series of questions. It is also known as the science of argument, or the science of dialogue, and works as the foundation of logic. The logic that we speak about in most conversations has its roots in this, but we don't always refer to it in the same way.

Logic and argument were so intricate to the Stoic pillars that they reformed language and the formula for a conversation to be able to transmit and analyze knowledge.

But this didn't happen in a sequential and urgent way. Socrates was not the founder of Stoicism, but he was the father of the logic and methods that led to its foundation almost a hundred years later.

The Socratic method, which we take for granted today, was not the norm in 400 BC. In fact, even toward the end of his life, the Socratic method had not become a mainstream discipline and only occurred after his passing thanks to his students, especially Plato.

As mentioned earlier, Socrates never wrote books or pamphlets. His main methods of research and the ideas he formulated were not memorialized by notes and texts but by teaching and discussing it with his students at the Agora.

Academy School of Thought

It was his student Plato, who under the auspices of Academy, a school he set up just outside Athens, who had refined Socrates' teachings and wrote about him. This Academy continued to breathe life into the words of Socrates and the concepts and methods he had developed in his lifetime. It also added to the conversation as Plato continued the tradition of exploration and development of the logic, reason, and methods of Socratic dialogue.

Socratic dialogue is an important element of Stoicism, even if it did predate the founding of the Stoa Poikile school by almost a century, and it is important that those who wish to understand the true nature of Stoicism understand the fundamentals or at least the methods by which the reasoning evolved up to that point.

Socratic dialogue is unlike other methods of knowledge distillation and synthesis. In comparison, a debate is heavily reliant on prose, oratory ability, and theatrics to some extent. It takes a short amount of time to get to the conclusion, but it leaves out important points that the lesser orator may have championed. In contrast, elections are inefficient. It has nothing to do with what is right, and worse, nothing to do with what is the truth. It is easier to conduct over a wide swath of participants, and for that reason, it serves its purpose in specific situations.

On the other hand, Socratic dialogue is more about reaching the truth. Socratic dialogue starts with a question, for example, "What is happiness?" From there a group of people get together and ask questions that penetrate deeper as they peel back each layer. Unlike balloting or debating, every question gets answered to the satisfaction of all before moving to the next layer. In this way, the topic is holistically viewed, and no gap is left to fester.

This was the process that led to Stoicism. It was from the Socratic dialogue that resulted in the idea of human existence and the distinction of human knowledge from human assumption. It is what first Plato's School, Academy, which, by the way, is the reason the name Academy applies to an institution of learning today.

However, Plato was not the only one to extend the mind and thoughts of Socrates to the next generation. Socrates just sparked the movement, and it took a hundred years of thought development beginning with his students Plato,

Euclid, Antisthenes, and Xenophon, and then advancing it to their students. From Plato, it passed to Xenocrates and Polemon, both heads of the subsequent iteration of Academy.

Megarians School of Thought

In parallel, while one vain of Socratic philosophy matured along the Academy track, Euclid of Megara, a mathematician, was developing a school of philosophy called the Megara. The Megarians School differed from Plato's Academy in many ways, but stylistically, it was more of a critique of the shortcomings of the other methods of getting to the truth.

A layer above that then it was one that was purely innovative. In the grand scheme of things, that is not a bad thing. It was actually a positive development at the time, and it went on to being a significant contribution to the development of Stoic philosophy, which was still at least eighty years away.

The Megarians brought another important piece of the puzzle to the table. They injected the part about goodness and wisdom. The Megarians contended that this good was an ethical imperative because they saw "good" as ethical and not as just a nicety.

In time they developed the ethical component of Socrates, and as the newer generations entered the Megarians, they introduced paradoxes into the conversation. To be clear, Aristotle and the Megarians clashed intellectually, which allowed the Megarians to further refine their stand, and that turned out to be a positive force in the eventual development of Zeno's Stoa Poikile.

From Euclid the baton passed to Thrasymachus of Corinth, and from him it went on to Stilpo, who progressed in the ethical development of Socratic philosophy in the Euclid's Megarians school. By the time Stilpo was teaching Megarians, it was almost a century since the passing of Socrates, and in that same span of time a third parallel track was being developed.

The Cynic School of Thought

This third track was that of the Cynics. Antisthenes, another student of Socrates, developed his own school of thought and proceeded to spread its teachings that were part of the mainstream before retreating around the time of the rise of Rome and then rising again a century later.

The Cynics are not what you think the word generally means in the English language. The Cynics are not ascetics contrary to some belief. Cynics tend to think that a life of virtue is one that is lived in agreement with nature. It is often mistaken to live in denial or live in exclusion of comforts as a way to punish one's self, but this is not entirely accurate. Cynics immerse their lives in the separation of self and comfort and do it as a way to retain clarity and piety.

One way to think of it is to see it as the life of absolute minimalism, where there are no forms of distractions and no desire to create disappointments. Between the three schools that erupted in the wake of Socrates' teachings, you can start to see that what came next after Zeno was almost the logical progression of what would happen. What, if anything, would minimalism have to do with any of the teachings of Stoicism? The answer is that Stoicism considers the distractions of daily desires and vanities to be something that can derail a person from what he is truly capable of and what he or she could otherwise achieve—true happiness. To be clear, it isn't the cessation of desire that brings the happiness but rather the errors and the emptiness that the fulfillment of these desires results in or the pursuit and lack of gaining release from those desires even after accomplishment.

One of the key elements of Antisthenes that passed on to his successors and even made it all the way to the founding of Stoicism was the notion of the brotherhood of man. The brotherhood of man he believed and espoused was far more important than any nationalistic or racial divide. No man was different based on the color of his skin, his port of origin, or his language.

From Antisthenes, the Cynic line came to Diogenes. For what seemed like excessive simplicity, he came to be known as the mad Socrates.

Diogenes took simplicity to a whole new level, believing that not only valuable and possessions were distractions but also were the more intangible acquisitions of vanity, power, prestige, and status. He reached the point where he would roam naked in the streets of Athens or just wearing a simple loincloth and lived in a barrel that was once used to store olive oil.

For food, he would beg in the marketplace, and, when needed, relieve himself by the side of the street. As reprehensible as this may sound, it signifies a man whose mind had no concern for whatever others thought of him. Eventually, his teachings became so popular and prominent that the Cynic school of thought was brought to the mainstream.

He was revered by others even though that reverence didn't bother him, as he viscerally did not include social appreciation or social structure and status as something that was worth inculcating.

When Alexander the Great once visited Athens and heard that Diogenes was close by, he hurried to meet him. When he got there, he found that Diogenes was sunbathing. He went to the Cynic and told him that whatever Diogenes wanted Alexander would grant it to him. Diogenes lifted his head, looked at Alexander, and said that all he wanted was the sunlight that Alexander was blocking at that moment. He was more interested in his dose of nature than anything the king could offer.

Alexander immediately moved away, and Diogenes went back to basking in the sun. Once leaving the market, Alexander commented to his entourage. "If I were not Alexander, I would like to be Diogenes." High praise from a king.

From Diogenes, the Cynic School passed to his student, Crates of Thebes. Crates was a wealthy man, and once he embraced the teachings of the Cynic School, he gave away all his possessions and lived on the streets of Athens along with his wife, who subscribed to his philosophy. He was also well respected in the city and constantly given food and consumables by passers-by. He lived the life dictated by the philosophy he believed in. His popularity resulted in a steady stream of students who wanted to live the life and find the secret to life that Crates seemed to have discovered. One of those men who wanted to understand his teaching was Zeno of Citium (Citium is pronounced "see-Shum").

Zeno of Citium

Zeno, born circa 336 BC, lived near present-day Larnaca in the southwestern part of Cyprus. Back then it was a Greek colony called Kition, an area with significant Semitic influence. Kition, in Latin, is Citium, thus Zeno of Citium. Zeno was the son of a rich merchant who frequently sailed back and forth across the Mediterranean and often stopped in Athens.

As Zeno matured, he was a voracious reader, and each time his father stopped in Athens he would pick up books for Zeno to read. Much of his reading at the time was focused on Plato's *Republic*, Xenophon's *Memorabilia*, and other texts by prominent writers of the time.

Before long, Zeno developed his own ideas and began to write at a young age before eventually joining his father in the family trade, where he would sail and learn the business until he was ready to set out on his own. Once he did, he would stop anytime he could in Athens to join different discussions and find more books to read.

On one of those occasions, he found a bookshop that carried many of the texts that intrigued him and more topics on Socrates, Plato, and even a treatise on Cynics, so he inquired as to where he could learn more. The Athenian bookseller pointed him across the street to Crates, who was sitting by the side of the street and mocking Athenian passers-by for their wealth and ignorance. Zeno was impressed.

Zeno was about thirty years of age at the time and was just a dozen years away from founding the Stoa Poikile. He joined Crates, and along with the teaching of Cynics, he continued to read up on the other veins of philosophy that had originally emanated from Socrates. Most importantly, he also looked at Plato's Academy and Euclid's Megarians.

The point to remember in all this is that Stoicism is the product of a century's worth of debate, discussion, and teaching that included the work product of various schools of thought.

Chapter 3 - Foundation of Stoic Philosophy

The Stoa that Zeno distilled from the amalgamation of Academic, Cynic, and Megarian schools of thought does not completely reflect the Stoicism that exists today, and it doesn't precisely embody the Stoa practiced by some segments of Imperial Rome during the time of Marcus Aurelius. They did, however, form the basis of it, which is why it is important to understand the evolution of Stoa so that the student of Stoicism can monitor the evolution in himself.

The foundations of the early Stoa principles came from various elements of the three schools of thought that flowed from the teachings of Socrates. At the same time, it was molded by disagreements with other schools of thought prevalent in Athens around the same period. These disagreements with other philosophies allowed the early proponents of Stoa to refine their own thoughts and ideas and to synthesize their position by articulating three guiding issues.

The first issue describes what the philosophy would be about. In the case of Stoa, the concept was about the ultimate happiness of man.

The second was about what predicated his ultimate happiness. In other words, what would one have to do to get to this point of being happy.

Finally, the third guiding issue was how the aforementioned happiness could be extended for a meaningful span of time rather than merely being a fleeting and superficial sort of pleasure or joy. In other words, the longevity of the actions and the echoes of its consequence as it meanders through the natural course of things.

By focusing on these three issues, what they uncovered through decades of argument and experiment was that it eventually touched on every aspect of a person's life. It was no longer just about the sensation of joy or the pain of suffering; it started to encroach into areas of thought, values, behavior, practices, and habits.

What the Stoics had come to realize is that the principles they were uncovering and espousing were the core values of what it meant to live a fulfilling life.

There was an alignment of the stars as well as far as the timing of all this was concerned. Athens was in the midst of tough financial conditions, and many impoverished citizens lived in and around the city. They needed hope, and philosophy was the only way they could see themselves marching out of the suffering that vexed their minds. Of all the schools of thought, they seemed to find it most in the teachings of Zeno of Citium.

The Stoic teachings that had been forged in the cauldron of a troubled Athens were accepted well, and they treated Zeno as a public hero, eventually erecting a statue in his honor in the marketplace and paying for his funeral when he died.

Zeno was not just a philosopher. He had spiritual and religious beliefs that were separate from mainstream thinking and beliefs of the day. Not many were teaching the kind of theistic matters that Zeno espoused, but he had the courage to think about them deeply and discuss them openly.

The fragment of his religious thought that made its way into Stoic philosophy (implicitly) was that he considered a monotheistic structure in divinity rather than a polytheistic truism that was the practice of the day. He had the courage to be considered a heretic. This was chiefly unlike anything that the Athenians or Greeks in general were accustomed to.

His twofold belief was that this monotheistic structure that paralleled Stoic philosophy was that of a single God of fatherly love who promoted brotherly spirit. This created something of a stir. In contrast to a polytheistic structure at the time, his alternative talked about one god that was omnipotent, omnipresent, and omnibenevolent.

He went on to say that the gods they worshiped, such as Athena and Poseidon, were mere manifestations of this single omnipotent god. It was revolutionary and started to take hold quietly. It was a philosophy based on something they felt warm about. They were not about to give up the religion of their ancestors, but the philosophy that he was espousing was at least acceptable because he didn't just disparage the current religious order but included it and gave it a larger context.

Besides, philosophy was not an affront to a belief in God in any way. He was lucky they didn't treat him as they did Socrates whom they accused of polluting the minds of youth with talks of an alternative worship structure.

In all, his Stoic beliefs had hues of spirituality without any hint of organized religion. By espousing Antisthenes' idea that all men are equal, without division of race and religion, he adopted a notion that he was a citizen of the world—something that has been lost in the narrative of the modern world we live in.

According to Zeno's reasoning, God was the father, and all men (denoting all humans) were brothers. If so, then the glue that holds us all together is love, not law. Mind you that this happened three hundred before another man from Galilee would preach the same thing to his followers.

But loving one's brother is not enough. It is just as easy to love someone but disrupt their lives from the preponderance of one's own ignorance. A mother may love her daughter, yet give her the wrong advice because she herself lacks the wisdom to know better. A father may steer his son wrong because he has failed to develop his own self-restraint. There are more areas in life than just love, which Zeno understood. That is the reason he brought more of Socrates' ideas into the Stoic school. Chief among them, he drew from Socrates' four areas of temperance, wisdom, courage, and justice.

To mold these four in the cast of Stoicism, he preached that the chief of the four cardinal virtues was wisdom. He believed that without wisdom the other three would fail. Thus, wisdom became the central product of conscious thought. But if wisdom was the core, then what gave rise to wisdom?

This is the obvious question that the students kept hounding Zeno about and he himself struggled to understand. Before long, it became obvious that aside from observation reason was the key element to build wisdom.

From there the Stoics had begun to purse all matters with reason and observation so that they could attain wisdom. To be able to use reason, they realized they had to alter their perception. They had to put their emotions on hold, and they had to pay attention to the details.

This framework pretty much still exists today. It is still widely accepted that Stoics are quiet individuals and fairly wise, although no Stoic will ever claim that he knows everything or that he is smart since he realizes one thing very early in his pursuit of wisdom—that it is difficult to know everything. The best we can hope for is to be part of a work in progress.

Stoic philosophy could not have spontaneously developed without the other schools of thought, which is why it is one of the most comprehensive and far-reaching philosophies to survive to the present day.

Fortunately, the Agora in Athens wasn't just filled with three or four groups. There were many more. Beyond the Cynics and the Academics, there were the Epicureans (the main opposition to Stoicism), Cyrenaics (pleasure seekers), and Peripateticism (Aristotle's school of thought) just to name a few. All of them had an impact on how Zeno and early Stoic thinking developed.

This was the Old Stoa—the Stoic values that were rapidly evolving and rapidly proliferating through the streets of Athens and the outlying city-states across Greece. The Old Stoa then slowed its rapid early evolution to a more gradual and organic pace as it resurfaced with vigor in the late first century BC. The chronological demarcation between the height of Old Stoa and the movement toward Middle Stoa occurred during the time of Chrysippus.

Chrysippus came to Athens from Soli in Cilicia, which is southern Turkey today. He was drawn by the teachings of the Stoic school of thought and studied under Cleanthes of Assos, who was Zeno's successor.

Although Cleanthes was a major force in the development of Old Stoa, his contributions were eclipsed by that of his student Chrysippus, who magnified and revolutionized the soul of Stoa by literarily adding to the teachings the *"pneuma"* of all things.

Pneuma in the context of philosophy refers to the air within us. For those who are students of etymology, you would probably recognize that pneuma has something to do with air in the English language. For instance, pneumatic has to do with mechanisms using compressed air.

In philosophy, pneuma was how the soul came to be described. Because the soul seems to have air like qualities in its invisibility and amorphousness, the closest one could describe these intangible phenomena was to equate it with air.

According to Chrysippus, pneuma was about the soul within us, and as fate would have it, it turned out that pneuma evolved into being the soul within Stoa. The inclusion of the concept of a soul marked the beginning of the Middle Stoa, which sparked renewed interest and carried it into pre-Imperial Rome.

By this point, Stoic philosophy had come to be a comprehensive school of thought that encompassed nature, belief, character, desires and pleasures, discipline, emotion, and the soul.

Then the story of Stoa went silent. There is not much documentation that reveals the status of Stoic proliferation at this point, but however silent the state of Stoic proliferation was it was just as widespread. By the turn of the epoch, Stoic values had begun to make their way to the outskirts of Greece, and that intersected with the provinces of Rome.

Circa 160 BC, a grammarian by the name of Crates of Mallus (not to be confused with Crates of Thebes mentioned earlier in this book) arrived in Rome. He was planning a short stay but broke his leg and had to extend his stay to convalesce. While there he began sharing his Stoic knowledge, and it seemed well received. If you are wondering what a grammarian has to do with Stoicism or its proliferation, it's understandable. Grammar was not part of linguistic priority in the pre-Greco period. The Stoics were the first to expound the importance of grammar so that language could be better used as a medium of communication. They wanted to deal in truth, and without precision or accuracy in language that would not be possible.

Once Crates of Mallus described his philosophy, it gained traction there but not by any significant degree. It wasn't until Panaetius of Rhodes, the last true Stoic scholar of Middle Stoa, arrived in Rome that Stoicism caught on with vigor. It happened that he was invited to join the Scipionic Circle. From there his influence spread to numerous other literary luminaries of the time in Rome, and that influence sparked a trend that saw his words enter the writings of Roman luminaires.

As a side note to the importance of Stoic principles, this anecdote is in order: The members of this literary circle appreciated the value of Panaetius' contribution to the furtherance of Stoicism in their midst and were voracious students of his instruction. Panaetius spent a large amount of his adult life in Rome before returning to Athens, but while in Rome he wrote a book on the topic duty, which is today one of the core tenets of Stoic philosophy. His writing on duty was then translated by Cicero himself who went on to title it *De Officiis*.

De Officiis became an iconic treatise among the educated and in the Christian church that was to come later. It was such a major piece of work that it was the second book printed by Johannes Guttenberg on his printing press after the Bible.

Roman Republic

Cato the Younger, circa 40 BC, started speaking of Stoa values in a society that was fast developing both in terms of military conquest and democratic institutions. The Romans had a central body to create laws, and these laws governed the formal conduct between the state and its citizens, between the citizens themselves, and for trade and commerce.

What was lacking in codified law was a framework of conduct that was beyond legislation, yet adhered to with the same fervor. This looser framework came to be known as the *mos moiorum*. Translated, it loosely means mores. In essence, the mores of a people dictate behavior and conduct that is acceptable and pervades deeper than laws could. There is no law that says one has to take care of one's parents when they grow old, but mores in many societies typically dictate that looking after them in their old age is a good thing to do, and society functions better. It is a minor example but one that should draw a distinction between legislation and practices.

By the time Cato the Younger was espousing this Greco philosophy on the streets of Rome and in the amphitheaters, Rome was facing a moral dilemma in that their mores were insufficient in advancing its vast empire.

Cato the Younger had a sister, Servile, who was the mistress of Julius Caesar and the mother of Brutus. Cato the Younger certainly had significant clout in Roman politics and philosophy, but his contributions were not just by bloodline and people he knew. He had significant intellect and morals along with a powerful sense of loyalty to the republic.

He saw the virtues of the Stoic philosophy as something that could supplement and buttress the mores of a growing Roman Republic, and he wasn't the only one who thought this way. Others wanted a better Rome, and Cato was definitely a patriot of the state of Rome and the ideals it represented.

Cato despised Julius Caesar and despised what would happen if Caesar disbanded the Senate and become emperor. He fought Caesar and sought to keep Rome in the hands of its people rather than live under a dictator. His thoughts on the matter were fodder and inspiration for such men as Benjamin Franklin and George Washington, who invoked Cato's words during the American Revolution.

The prolific biographer Plutarch tells us in *Life of Cato* that Cato was a genius in his youth and immensely socially conscious. He exhibited a profound understanding of social concerns and realized that a man's life was made worthy by his contribution.

His ideals did not sprout in a vacuum. Many of his ideals had been part of his grandfather's words. His grandfather was Cato the Elder and also an ardent student of Stoic philosophy.

His study of Stoic values directed Cato the Younger to live a modest lifestyle even though he hailed from a wealthy family and was successful in his own endeavors. The idea was not to remain poor but to live modestly.

Cato the Younger understood clearly that distractions are the path to unhappiness and the fruit of desires, materialism, and pleasures of the flesh. Most tenets of Stoic philosophy came naturally to Cato, and so when he started studying Stoicism it resonated within him naturally.

It was here that Stoicism revived to its higher phase, and this was the start of the New Stoicism. Cato's contribution to Stoic values was a ramped-up sense of duty. Just as Chrysippus modeled Stoicism to include a soul, Cato brought out the sense of duty to its purpose.

With Cato's contribution, the Stoic story had come to be a coherent and robust philosophy that appealed to the higher minds of the Roman world. Even though he was not able to prevent the dictatorship of Rome, he did manage to inject the virtues of happiness, the existence of a soul, and the purpose of duty into the Stoic saga that entered the Roman Empire.

Roman Empire

As Rome advanced under the dictatorship of Julius Caesar and then grew under the direction of the emperors after him, Stoicism gained footing and became part of the mainstream. It had a hand in the thoughts, culture, mores, and legislation that grew from the subsequent iterations of Stoic values and the new Stoic framework that began to exhibit a more Roman flavor. Just as religion today is dictated by the culture it spreads across, philosophy and culture behave the same way.

Hence, the Stoic school of thought began to develop a more Roman vein, and most of the readings, thoughts, and guidelines we find today are of Roman flavor since some of the writers who are popular today were Romans.

Many Romans carried the Stoic torch that was first lit by Panaetius and on to Cato the Elder and his grandson, Cato the Younger. From there it carried on unceremoniously and spread across the Roman provinces, but, more importantly, it penetrated the mind of the Roman citizen to a deeper level. It became the philosophy of the illuminated and the ideals of the patriot.

It had become so ingrained in Roman heritage that by the time Constantine had commissioned the collation and creation of the Bible there was a strong Stoic presence within him and the members who were involved in the collation of the Bible. Stoicism indeed had been a driving force of the Romans who stitched together elements of existing religion with elements of Stoic philosophy to come up with a coherent religion that could go on to dominate the minds of Romans.

Once the adoption of Christianity was complete, Emperor Justinian I abolished the teaching of Stoicism in Rome. With Christianity as the state-sponsored religion, it became illegal for philosophers or naturalists to express their ideas of divinity, and Stoicism had to dive underground. Until now.

Chapter 4 - Observing Nature

"All worldly things thou must behold and consider, dividing them into matter, form, and reference, or their proper end."

— **Meditations, Emperor Marcus Aurelius Antoninus Augustus, 180AD**

With its history behind us and an understanding of how Stoic philosophy unfolded, it's now necessary to lay the foundation of the concept of nature as a Stoic sees it. The nature of all things is directly tied to the other veins that run through Stoic virtues and Stoic philosophies, and understanding it will go a long way for understanding Stoicism.

We will explore nature by visualizing it in different ways to see what it is and what it is not.

A powerful way to visualize nature is to observe a symphony in progress. The overall melody produced by the musicians is composed of individual sounds and rhythms layered atop each other and chain-linked in a specific combination.

Each layer of instruments may have its own melody and cadence. For instance, the wind section may be doing one thing, while the brass and strings may be doing something else. The symphony of more than a hundred different instruments coming together creates a deep and rich experience, even if, individually, their notes, tempo, and even volume are all different at any one time. Not all the instruments from percussions to wind and strings are playing the same musical note. Yet, when they come together, the objective is accomplished.

In the same way, the universe is like the symphony. This universe is not one infinitely large phenomena. It is the amalgam of a countless number of singularities that exist individually, just like the symphony. We don't need to look at the various components to understand the whole, but we do need to at least see the whole in a way that allows us to realize that what we see is not all there is. It would be naïve to listen to a recording of a performance and think that just one instrument made the melody.

But it goes further than that regarding the universe.

In addition to the layers that are detectable to our senses, there are layers that are not. Just because you can't see waves of gravity emanating from the earth and holding the moon in its grip does not mean they aren't there.

Just because you can't see atoms and molecules does not mean they aren't there. You know they exist because you've learned in school that particles smaller than what your eyes can detect do exist, but the exact nature of those atoms and molecules are not apparent to us. We don't even know the truth about them. The models that we use are just best guesses and seem to work well under most conditions, so we take them to be adequately true.

For instance, the atomic model that most of us are used to looks like planets orbiting the sun. In reality, they are not like that at all. For one thing, they orbit in a three-dimensional orbit, and the plates orbit in a two-dimensional orbit. The idea is easy to communicate, however, and works in most situations. If you use this model and just use your eyes to see it, you will be deceived and not grasp the truth.

Our senses can only detect one layer—a superficial one. That layer is limited in scope. When you observe something with your eyes, it is only limited to the amount of light that is present, and since light cannot bend, you can only see the side that is facing you. You also can't see the light that is beyond the visual spectrum, so if there are any electromagnetic emanations from the object you are observing, you would not be able to detect them. As such, you are limited to what you see in terms of dimension and frequency, not more. If the object is at a distance, then you are also probably limited by the fact that you can't hear it, can't smell it, and can't touch it. That makes it even more indiscernible.

The only way you can observe it and make sense of it is to cogitate, observe the effects, and postulate its nature using the faculties of your mind. In other words, you need your mind to observe. That is the essence of the Stoic—to observe with the mind.

Sight, sound, smell, touch, and taste. Anything beyond this—any object beyond our visual range—is invisible to us, and sound beyond our audible range is silent to us, and smell that is too minimal for our olfactory sense to detect is nonexistent to us, and any texture too fine for us is rendered indistinguishable.

This is what Einstein meant when he said that "Imagination is more important than knowledge." He was not referring to the fantasy of the mind or the flittering daydreaming that brings us virtual pleasures. He was talking about the mind's ability to see past what it knows by looking deep into the nature of things. This is the man that imagined the existence of black holes and imagined that time changes as one speeds up or slows down. This is the imagination of a Stoic.

A Stoic understands the world around him because he is not limited to observing with only his senses but subjects it to his enquiring mind.

In other words, you see with your mind, not your eyes; you hear with your mind, not your ears; you taste with your mind, not your tongue; you smell with your mind, not your nose; and you feel with your mind, not your touch.

When you do that, as the Stoic does, you get a deeper sense of understanding in all that you come into contact with, and you begin to absorb the event holistically. That allows you to understand the nature of the object or the event.

Stoicism is a philosophy, not a religion. When you look to understand Stoicism, there must be a reason behind it. You are probably in search of its philosophy or its guidance. That's a good place to start, but it is not a good way to proceed. To come in search of it so that it can end on a better path for you is a good motivation, but you can't meaningfully advance if you think that Stoicism is about to give you a set of rules— human algorithms that would magically give you happiness and insight. It won't. However, Stoicism is about practicing the ability to observe and understand nature, and then you will be able to harvest the wisdom that that offers so that you can then execute the duty that you are uniquely designed to accomplish.

In Stoicism, there is no destination, only the journey. The nature of things is not definable by algorithms, formulas, and step-by-step instructions. It is something that your mind has to observe and penetrate. The defining characteristic of a Stoic is that he develops his mind to see the nature and character of objects and events.

The Stoic drills deeper and observes and then absorbs how all things behave and their nature. In the process, the Stoic is made aware of two things: (1) he is a part of all things that are around him and (2) he must go beyond his senses to be able to take advantage of all the powers and all the benefits that he is entitled to.

This is one reason why the Cynics and other schools of thought that also figured this out realized that they were in search of something much more than just the fleeting pleasures of the flesh. From adulation and respect to fine robes and rich food, the Cynics realized that these factors blunted their ability to sharpen their mind and cultivate their wisdom.

The Stoics are well aware of that but seek to balance the extremes of meager living, and even though it is highly unlikely that you will drop everything and resign to live in a barrel like Diogenes the Cynic or on the streets like Zeno of Citium, you should still contemplate the reason others before you have done so. This contemplation shouldn't lead you to the same actions but instead lead you to the outcome they were searching for.

Stoicism is not about an endeavor that seeks external poverty and internal solemnity. Stoics do not wish to embrace asceticism. The Stoic does not blindly enter a state of poverty but does so with a specific goal to sharpen his mind by dulling his base desires.

Coming back to the symphony, when you attempt to deconstruct the melody, the sequence, and the layers, you find that it gives you endless hours of insight into a number of things that you never thought possible. There are the individual instruments, there is the relationship between pairs and groups of instruments, there is the tempo of the instruments, and also the pitch that it rises to or falls toward. Then there is the volume and the undulating loudness and silence of the piece. They are all different dimensions that you find in one piece of music or even in a single movement. Then you take it from there and realize that each sound when represented on its own means little, yet when placed together means so much.

More importantly, with that particular arrangement of sound, when there is the sequence of strings to percussions or the particular sequence of notes, something happens that only you can feel within you. You either feel elation, sadness, happiness, or darkness. There is an interaction between something that comes in a million different dimensions, and then it affects you in a way that is inexplicable.

What you are experiencing at that point is the layer of nature, and that is what you want to see in everything around you, and that is what a Stoic sees when he observes.

When you think about nature, it helps to think about the symphony and how all the individual parts function, and then the overarching result comes about, seemingly all by itself.

A person's character is the same way. There are countless individual traits, habits, ideals, and assumptions that play on their own, resulting in the nature of a person. This is what we call character. After a lifetime of contemplation, meditation, and reflection, a Stoic aligns all his parts until his nature is aligned perfectly toward his duty. At this point, he achieves his fullest measure of happiness.

Chapter 5 - Balancing Distractions in Pursuit of Purpose

"If it be not fitting, do it not. If it be not true, speak it not. Ever maintain thine own purpose and resolution free from all compulsion and necessity."

— Meditations, Emperor Marcus Aurelius Antoninus Augustus, 180AD

The human mind and consequently the human condition is one that is constantly trying to find a sense of balance. Think about it this way: if you are famished, you are driven to eat as much as you can. As you proceed to fill up, the desire that you had to eat gradually diminishes until you get to a point where there is no longer any driving desire.

Each step of that driving desire that is fulfilled (by eating) is rewarded by the sense of pleasure that you feel. When you feel that pleasure or results in a desire in the future to feel that pleasure, that is the basis of a habit.

Yes, eating is a habit. It's not a habit in a way that you may think of smoking or waking up and brushing your teeth, but it is a pattern that is developed based on a desire the body gives you, the fulfillment of that desire, and the reward for fulfilling it. Eating, just like smoking, drugs, or anything else that makes you want to do something, is considered a habit.

The sequence is fairly simple. It starts with a desire. You fulfill the requirements of the desire. You are then rewarded, and that reward makes you feel good. That good feeling makes you remember. So, the next time the trigger of hunger is issued, you are compelled to satisfy it and collect the reward. It is the natural mechanism of the body, and it applies to many ways your body gets you to do things.

That part of things is fine, but things start to go awry when you start forcing the pleasure of reward rather than the underlying need. Stoics shun pleasure not because they are boring people but because they do not want to create a habit and do things because their bodies feel like it.

That is what suffering is made from—the inability to satisfy a desire. Stoics find that suffering is a distraction and, as such, they nip the problem in the bud by addressing the issues of desire.

If you apply the proper discipline and understanding, then that wisdom will allow you to fulfill what needs to be done without the need of being a response to a desire.

If you are disciplined and know when to apply it, you will be able to avoid the trappings of desire and pleasure. That would consequently help you control your emotions.

The Human Need for Emotion

There are two sides to human consciousness. One is reasoned and logical, while the other is emotional and seemingly rash. There are just as many benefits to both as there are flaws inherent to each. To be able to understand the rationale behind Stoicism, we need to look at the emotional aspect of our existence so that we can see how it plays with the rational side.

What is emotion? Is it the urge to cry when things go wrong? Is it the feeling that one is overwhelmed with when one is elated or depressed? What are the characteristics of emotions? Are they valid? These are the kinds of things that you should think of when you are trying to understand the meaning of emotions.

Emotions are not feelings. Emotions are the biochemical responses you have to an event. Feelings are what tell your consciousness that an emotion is triggered. When you break down your psyche, you will find that these feelings of emotions can often be distracting.

There are a number of reasons behind the distractions and the obscuration caused by these emotions. For one thing, the core emotion and the feeling that it triggers can be quite strong, and that will automatically take up the mind's processing ability and render other functional thoughts almost incoherent. It's like it would be impossible for you to solve a math problem if you were being taunted by a bear at the same time. Your mind instantly directs its thoughts to the more pressing matter.

Distinguishing Feeling from Emotion

The feeling of fear, apprehension, and anxiety can be extremely distracting, and if you are in the midst of an anxiety attack, you will quickly realize that there is no way for you to be able to cogently and coherently think about anything.

Feelings are the sensations you feel if something is going on within you. They are a little more than just the tactile sensations that you detect when a light breeze grazes you or when drops of rain soak you. This kind of feeling is not about the tactile input that you experience.

Take it one step further. When you are hungry, do you know it, feel it, or notified about it? What is that sensation? Which internal mechanism alerts you of something going on inside you? Think about that. Identify the mechanism within you through introspection and you will find that there are different components to it. To take an extreme example, imagine if you felt a hunger sensation but you were suddenly chased by a rabid dog. Would you still feel that hunger sensation while you were running? Does that mean your body's need for nutrition is diminished or you just stopped feeling it?

When you feel a sensation of admiration, when the hair on the nape of your neck stands in fear, when you feel anxiety, fear, joy, sadness, trust, or even disgust, that sensation is not entirely a natural response. It is learned. It is learned through experience and so is the response to that experience. It's all learned, and it can be unlearned.

Stoics make the effort to look into themselves to understand the connection between a sensation and the way that sensation is felt. It is a process of getting to know one's self. Remember the Roman saying "Conquer yourself and you conquer the world."

When you respond to a certain event, that response is based on a string of subconscious processes all of which are learned and then internalized. The first is the perception of the event. How you perceive that event determines the range of choices you have. A response is still not part of the process, but it will be based on a range of choices that you have in that subset. So, for instance, if you are empathic, you have a certain range of choices to a given event. That same event will have a different set of choices to a sociopath. As an empath, if you see a child crying because it has lost its parents, you may start to feel an intense sense of pain, but the sociopath will not feel a thing.

That frame of existence will then determine how each person responds. A Stoic does not feel bad when he sees a child cry. That doesn't make him a sociopath. A Stoic, instead, gets to his feet and does something about it if he can. If he can't, he moves on without feeling bad about not doing anything. Action is more important than feeling.

That feeling you get or don't get indicates the sensation that results after this string of perception, experience, and foresight of what may happen next. If you stay in the moment, like being in a snapshot of an event, that event in itself is incapable of rendering any particular sensation and thus no discernable feeling.

Staying in the Moment

A powerful way to balance your emotions and rewire your feelings is to remain in the moment and not project forward or regress into history. The Buddhists call it being mindful of the present.

Stoics see the present as the most valuable of all moments in time. In the present, anything is possible; in the past, you have no control; and the future is impossible to control without setting the events of the present into motion.

When a Stoic stays in the moment, he does it for three reasons. The first one is related to the balancing of emotions because in the present the ability to balance an emotion is ideal.

One can't change something in the past, so an emotion can't be countered. In the future, the events can't be altered unless you change the present, so the emotions presuming the future are a waste of time. That leaves us with the emotions triggered by events of the present, and it is very easy to dilute them with actions you can take to address the underlying cause of the emotion and subsequent feeling.

The Stoic equation is clear in this respect. If you stay in the moment, you are able to do whatever is necessary to handle the issue that is causing a negative emotion and thus a negative feeling. What you cannot do is get caught up with the feeling, and then no one is left in the driver's seat to take the necessary action to counter the emotion with a neutralizing action.

Imagine a deer in the headlights. The deer freezes because of the fear of impending doom. The key word here is "impending." It hasn't happened yet. The deer is afraid of something that is about to happen, but the Stoic knows that if energy is diverted to thinking of a solution rather than freezing a better outcome is more likely.

That's the benefit of staying in the moment

The most common feeling is the feeling of fear. One is afraid of what may happen if he or she were to lose their job. They are not afraid that they may have lost their job in the present. You are afraid of what may happen to your children if they don't do well in school, not that they are not doing well now. Our fear is a projection of what (we think) is going to happen in the future. That fear, the emotion, and the feeling are distractions to solving the problem.

Perception

The next factor in the destruction of emotion is the learned responses to the perception of that event. Say, for example, if you perceive someone is going to harm you, you will not wait to begin preparing your defense.

Perceptions are not reality, but they dictate the subsequent reality of what will happen. Stoics do not give perceptions the weight of truth. They consider perceptions frivolous and would rather deal in truth. In the absence of the ability to discern the truth of the matter, they withhold action and response. It is better to do nothing than to react poorly to the wrong perception.

Stoics spend a lifetime in pursuit of observing the truth. Even master negotiators today use these Stoic skills in ascertaining their counterparts' meaning and intentions.

Wrong perceptions lead to poor expectations and unnecessary escalations in the wrong direction, resulting in suboptimal outcomes.

Balancing Expectations

One aspect of Stoic wisdom comes from balancing expectations. Stoics don't walk into a situation with expectations that are counterproductive. Instead, they do all they can to see things the way they are so that the course of events that eventually unfolds is as close to the path that the Stoic has deduced based on fact and reason.

As part of those reason and fact patterns, Stoics realize that they have to work for the best but expect the worst. In all the possible combinations of work and expectation, they have to cover all their bases and work with the facts and endeavor to reach an outcome but expect the worse.

By expecting the worst, they are not blindsided and left like a deer in the headlights when things don't go their way. Expecting the worst also allows them to divert more resources and efforts toward an objective.

Expecting the worst is what gets Stoics off their laurels and their nose to the grindstone. It is the primary reason behind most Stoics winning the day.

Think about Emperor Marcus Aurelius' following words and how they pertain to expectations:

> "Begin the morning by saying to thyself, I shall meet with the busy-body, the ungrateful, arrogant, deceitful, envious, unsocial. All these things happen to them by reason of their ignorance of what is good and evil. But I who have seen the nature of the good that it is beautiful, and of the bad that it is ugly, and the nature of him who does wrong, that it is akin to me, not only of the same blood or seed, but that it participates in the same intelligence and the same portion of the divinity, I can neither be injured by any of them, for no one can fix on me what is

ugly, nor can I be angry with my kinsman, nor hate him, For we are made for co-operation, like feet, like hands, like eyelids, like the rows of the upper and lower teeth. To act against one another then is contrary to nature; and it is acting against one another to be vexed and to turn away."

This paragraph comes from the beginning of Book Two. You can consider it to be the second chapter of his book *Meditations*. If you understand the history of this book, you will know that Marcus Aurelius did not intend for the book to be published. It was a compilation of his thoughts and philosophy.

He was a modern-day Stoic at the time and had written much of his thoughts and observations in a way that he could read it back to himself during those long journeys and times when he needed his own counsel.

There are two things we can learn from this. If we practice the art of journaling, it will allow us to make more effective use of our lessons in life, but that is not the point of this chapter, which is:

To be able to control the way you respond to things requires that you invoke a certain kind of mind-set so that you will not be distracted or create the wrong perception and then go down a path that reduces your ability to get out of negative consequences.

It turns out that because the human mind is so susceptible to perception and perception is so susceptible to experience it creates a seemingly endless loop. Those who are born into a life of hardship perceive things to always be hard. They can't help it. Those who are born into a life of wealth think differently. A wealthy man, born with a silver spoon, defines a bad day very differently from a man who is born into poverty. That perception creates a reinforcing effect.

On the other hand, it is not just about how one sees himself. It's also about how one sees others. If one is raised to believe in a negative perception of people of certain looks, then whenever they see that person there will be some level of trepidation. The perception-consequence-experience link is indelibly linked unless you take the time to break it through contemplation and reflection.

You may wonder if it helps to start the day as Marcus Aurelius suggests by thinking that someone is going to bug you or be off color to you. The reason he advocates this method is so that you prepare yourself and strengthen your perception rather than fall into it.

Stoics study everything in granular detail so that they can understand the nature of everything, including the nature of emotion, perception, habit, and desire. There is widespread understanding of a person's desire, but it is also important to remember that Stoics realize they need to look inside to understand their own emotion and what triggers it so that they can master themselves.

Having these kinds of expectations will eventually affect your perceptions. This results in your ability to control your outcomes, and that creates your bulk of experiences. If you control your expectations and your outcomes are good, then that creates positive reinforcement.

If you expect someone is going to be bad but you are pleasantly surprised that they are good, all is well. That saves you from a poor experience and allows you to have a better perception in the future.

Expectations and Emotions

Tempering emotion will allow you to see things as they are and to live life as it is really intended to be.

This world is built on the principle of equity and consequence. If you drop a ball, regardless of whether it was intentional or accidental, that ball is going to fall to the ground. It will not miraculously float away and not knock over what is beneath it. You can't wish that away, and you cannot prevent it from happening.

Emotion, however, is something that can be controlled and be an obstacle if it's not controlled. Emotions distract you from seeing the real issue and understanding the nature of what you are observing. Stoics see emotion as a barrier against effective understanding.

We have talked about fear being an emotion that is a projection in the future. There is a very specific reason for that. It is part of our defense mechanism to be able to predict what consequence can happen in the future based on what action we undertake.

If that action is detrimental, then we can expect a consequence that is detrimental. At that point, the mind begins to observe associative features. The mind doesn't just notice the action. It notices the consequences of those actions. "If I release a ball, it falls toward the ground." The next time I don't want the ball to fall toward the ground I make sure I do not release it, and if I want the ball to drop to the ground, then I release it. It is a learned sequence of consequence. Until you experience gravity, you won't know if the ball will drop or how quickly it will drop when you release it.

It's also one of the things that Stoics are not afraid of—they are not afraid to make mistakes because they can learn from them. If you didn't know gravity existed, the first time you released something and it fell, you will learn very quickly that something is pulling the object to the ground. You learn from mistakes, and you learn for getting it right. In essence, you learn from doing. Stoics are not just deep thinkers and observers; they are also doers who reflect on every action from which they can learn.

Emotions and expectations block that experience because they raises the ante by giving you a negative feeling in the pit of your stomach when you don't accomplish your objective.

Expectations and Probability in Stoicism

There is an added layer in the human mind that is built on expectations. What if the expectation is that you do not allow that ball you are holding to fall to the ground, and you know if you do not release the ball it won't fall to the ground, so you should be able to control your destiny with that ability to predict consequences.

But a funny thing happens inside the untrained mind, which has to do with probability. Stoics were some of the first philosophers in the later years to start looking at how probability and the mind started to affect the mind's perception of the outcome and how it anticipated the trajectory of events. There is the probability of known possibilities and the probability of unknown possibilities.

All events that have yet to happen are subject to one of many trajectories. You either know what the trajectory will be to account for it, or you realize that there are trajectories that could come from outside your range of projections.

The mind is a powerful calculator, and it will crunch the numbers and put you in one state or another without you even having to do the math. If the subconscious mind has all the necessary information and knows the calculus, it will run the numbers and give you a sense of what the possibilities are.

However, when you can't crunch the numbers because the mind doesn't have the necessary figures, it is designed to err on the side of caution. It looks at two factors. The first is that it looks at the probability of harm or failure, and then it looks at the consequence of failure.

The more adverse the consequence, the lesser appetite the mind has for even low levels or probable failure. If the consequences are minuscule or nonexistent, then the mind computes that it can afford to take on a higher amount of probable risk.

Look at it this way. Let's say you are playing blackjack and playing with fake money. How much will you bet on the cards you have? You could bet the farm and not worry about it because it's fake. You have nothing to lose. What if you have a winning hand with just a 13% chance of losing? Would you still bet the farm? What if you have an average hand and a 60% chance of losing? Would you still bet large?

Stoics understand that the probability of an event is an important factor in what happens, and so they pay close attention to the nature of things because it is the nature of things that allows us to peer into the world of probability and outcome.

The higher the chances of losing, the less you will be inclined to make a significant bet. The mind works in the same way. The more it sees the chances of a failure, the more it backs off in making the bet. Adversity and consequence are evaluated in this fashion. The higher the cost of failure, the lower your tolerance for it becomes. The lower the cost of failure, the more you are willing to take a risk even if that chance of risk is high.

How does this show up in your conscious mind? It shows up with the emotion of fear and anxiety, which will not harm you but will cause your expectations to be unfulfilled. In the Stoic's mind then, the way to destroy that sense of fear and the emotion that is being felt because of it is to abolish expectations.

Putting it Together

Putting it all together, it is easy to see how most Stoics do well in life and not just in monetary terms. They do well in life in the way they approach things and the decisions they make because they have realized the ability to take the risk in a way that can be effectively mitigated, and then they win. Winners are those who know that wealth can only be built when risk is taken.

In essence, you have to alter your risk appetite and bring it down to almost zero. That is what Stoics endeavor to do and in most cases are successful. They reduce their fears of a future event by understanding that event and then altering the actions so that a series of consequences do not alter their trajectory. When you know the nature of things, you face reduced chances of failure.

To alter your risk appetite, you need to alter your emotional profile. Once you can alter your emotions and assign them to the correct areas of your life, then you will find that you are able to apply logic to all that you do, and the outcome and consequences of your actions create a better path forward.

You are not required to abolish your emotions. Emotions serve a critical purpose in your life, but you need to be able to differentiate when it is a useful form or where it is a distraction and then tone it down so that you are able to think clearly and wisely. Stoics do not abolish emotions but rather take their input into advisement.

If you can only be one or the other, then be logical and thoughtful, but if you have the ability to be balanced, then you will find that applying Stoic principles to bona fide emotional tendencies can give you superior outcomes. To do that, Stoics control the vagrancies and excesses of emotions.

The problem with keeping emotions in the picture is that you end up getting used to allowing it to determine your actions. If you could keep your emotions online but keep them in check, then you will find that you have better outcomes.

When you have emotion and logic constantly working, one of the things that can be observed from the outside is that you are silent and pensive. A Stoic is constantly silent so that he or she can divert the necessary resources to balance their logic and emotion.

The destruction of emotion is not the total annihilation of emotion. You need to break it down so that it does not ride roughshod over your conscious logic and subconscious intuition.

Chapter 6 - Practicing Silence

"Be silent for the most part, or, if you speak, say only what is necessary and in a few words. Talk, but rarely, if the occasion calls you, but do not talk of ordinary things—of gladiators or horses races or athletes or of meats or drinks— these are topics that arise everywhere—but above all do not talk about men in blame or compliment or comparison. If you can, turn the conversation of your company by your talk to some fitting subject; but if you should chance to be isolated among strangers, be silent."

— Epictetus

To use our mind to contemplate the observations we make, we need to set the environment in our mind to be as silent and still as possible. It is almost like looking at one's reflection in a pond. If the pond is in chaos and there are ripples ricocheting from the banks, the reflection will not appear with any real clarity, but if you wait and allow the ripples to dissipate, then the reflection will be significantly clearer.

To be able to do this, we need to be able to manage the silence that is required because the simile of the ripples in the pond describes different lives of silence that a Stoic gradually becomes adept with over the course of his practice.

Silence exists on two levels. First, there is mechanical silence that is created by the cessation of mechanical sound, which is what your ears detect and what your voice creates. This exists on a tangible level and can be altered, created, and silenced.

Then there is intangible silence, which is rather different from mechanical silence in many ways. It is not something that you can shatter with sound. Neither is it something that you can put your finger on directly because you can't capture it with any of your five senses. To imagine intangible sound, just imagine reading the text you are reading right now in a way that feels as if you are reading it in your head. It almost seems that you can hear it, but in actual fact, your ears are not playing any part in this. It's all in your mind.

That's intangible sound.

The mechanical and tangible properties of sound are picked up by one specific sense in the human body—the ears. That is then sent to the auditory cortex for processing before being sent to the amygdala to be encoded and referenced.

Intangible sound has no corresponding sensor in the body like the ears. Your ears, nose, eyes, tongue, and skin can't detect it. That is why it is thought of and described as an intangible phenomenon. It is conjured purely in the mind, and it is something that can be voluntary or involuntary.

When it is voluntary, it is like when we read in silence. When it is involuntary, it is the random thoughts that bounce around in our head. Those are the thoughts that we "hear" and are analogized by the ripples in the pond that continuously bounce off each other. We have no direct control over this, and that requires that we have a strategy to silence it and control it to be able to get to a deeper part of ourselves.

The two kinds of silence are connected at a point that is consequential to the discussion of Stoicism and the practice of observation, reflection, contemplation, and meditation. For mechanical silence to exist, it does not mean that we need to stop all sound around us and cover our ears or enter a soundproof room. A deeper intangible silence needs to be at its core. Without that silence, the mechanical silence will fall in failure; in other words, it will not last.

Stoics learn to control their minds and the conscious process to be able to control the ripples in the pond. The reason it can seem rather daunting for the uninitiated to endeavor to silence the mind is that there are three factors at play.

- The mind's insistence to listen and react to any sound in the world around us. (external distractions)

- The mind's chatter of thoughts that keep triggering based on association. (internal distractions)

- The priority of the thoughts that arise, by association, and derails the mind from being in the moment. (matters of priority)

Practicing silence is a way to neutralize all three factors, and it resides in the core of the Stoics' abilities to get to the truth of all matters.

Strategies to Still the Mind

To start the process, it is helpful for a person to make the conscious decision to reduce the chatter in the mind. To do this, the best aspect of silence to control is the aspect of generating more sound pollution by reducing how much is spoken. The less one speaks, the less the mind is triggered into other associated thoughts and corresponding emotions.

If you are going to be doing this for the first time, get away for the day and go someplace where you can't be reached. Turn off your devices and step into a new environment.

Practicing Stoics today do this periodically, where they turn off electronic devices and unplug from the chaos that may seem like nothing but will creep up on you and disturb your peace.

Parks, nature walks, lakes, and such are good candidates to change your environment when you are doing this for the first time. Such environments will arrest all the tangible sounds that you can control. These tangible sounds that you can turn off or walk away from are the first layer in calming the ripples of the mind.

The sounds that we subject ourselves to, from the music we love to the barking of the annoying dog down the street, are all distractions that tug at the fabric of our peace and set our minds off on a tangent from where it needs to be.

When we silence the distractions that we can control, it releases the mind that has been consciously and even to a certain extent subconsciously locked on to and overwhelmed by it. That consequently affects the thoughts triggered by association—the ripples mentioned earlier.

These thoughts, or thought fragments, that are triggered by association are something we can't control directly. We can diminish them by controlling the tangible sounds that trigger them, and when you extract yourself from the chaos, it goes a long way in accomplishing this. Additionally, when you start to focus on the subsequently diminishing levels of sound, you are actively fencing your mind from the sounds that would otherwise cause those ripples to manifest.

This strategy is a significant part of the process and deserves repeated practice, but it doesn't end here. If you recall, there are three sources of distractions in the mind that we are concerned with in this chapter. We just reviewed the first.

The second involves thoughts that the mind generally throws up on its own. You don't have to consciously trigger a thought, but in a disquiet mind, thoughts have the habit of popping up on their own, and those random thoughts then cascade into a series of other associative thoughts.

These are part of what we also call intangible sounds. You can almost hear these thoughts in your head, and you can almost detect the responses as your conscious mind argues, debates, or converses to quell them or jumps in to agree with them.

When you stop the mechanical sounds, you have accomplished a lot to reduce the intangible sounds, but some of these will still be there. It's a point in time that you will reach to seemingly freeze the chaos around you but not necessarily the sounds within you, which you can't control.

That's when it's time to try a trick that will sweep over you with astonishing freshness. Listen to all the sounds that you can't control—e.g., the sounds of the trees rustling, the sound of the occasional car passing by, sounds of people walking. Focus on them one at a time. Train yourself to consciously hunt and target these sounds and then isolate them.

Find the sound that is most obvious in that environment and pay attention to it. Once you identify and hone in on it and have a good hold on that sound, move to the next obvious sound.

Keep working toward the least obvious sound until there is no other sound that is fainter. Once you are able to go lower and lower to the faintest of sounds, what's beyond that is the silence.

If you are not doing this outdoors, you could simulate this exercise by listening to a single symphony and instead of isolating the sounds of nature, you could isolate the sounds of individual instruments. If you are doing the exercise using music, pick one that has no vocals and preferably pick one that is orchestral. In my experience, one of the best pieces to do this is the first movement in Beethoven's Symphony 9.

Once you learn to pay attention to the individual components of the cacophony of sounds that are around you, your mind will automatically realize what each sound is and that they are unique components of the whole rather than just a droning hum in the background. The mind is powerful this way. Once you pay attention to it, they are no longer a blanket of anonymous sounds that you may find challenging to isolate. Paying attention to them changes your interaction with them and allows you to turn them lower (or completely turn them off) one at a time until they all fade away.

By the time you get to the last sound, you realize that it has been a very active process. There is nothing passive about the art of concentrating or the art of excluding distractions.

Once you get to the last sound and pull that down, what you are left with is silence, and because you have approached this gradually, you will find that you will be able to lock onto it. If you keep practicing this, over time you will find that you are able to identify the silence in the most chaotic of places and focusing on that.

If you lose your grip on it, just go back to looking for that last sound that you were focusing on before getting to the silence, and then start to find that silence that you locked onto from there.

That is the strategy for the second of three situations that we talked about earlier in the chapter. The strategy to arrest the third factor in controlling the ripples in one's mind is fairly straightforward and will be easily accomplished if you have already managed to get the last two strategies to work.

It would be a good idea for you to practice getting to this point for two main reasons. The first is that it will allow you to take baby steps to a practice that is rather daunting if you have not done it before or if you have tried and found that it is quite impossible to focus on silence.

Even though we look at it in baby steps, practicing silence is really an art and not a science. It comes with practice.

Finally, we come to the strategy for the third factor that involves reprioritizing your mind-set. This is a longer-term strategy and one that is iterative. It involves the rewiring of your brain and reprioritizing of issues that you deem important but is, in fact, not critical. There are common troves of misconception that lurk around one's brain, and most of it has to do with some form of fear. It is the reason behind the runaway anxiety that people face.

While all this is what we have talked about as intangible sounds and the thoughts that spring from within your mind, these anxious feelings are ones that you can viscerally feel in the pit of your stomach. In some people, it can be mild, while in others it can be violent.

This book is not about methods to control one's anxiety, but it is worth noting that involuntary or irrational anxiety is common and can be a major distraction to those on the path to practice Stoic values.

Stoicism, it is worth remembering, is best practiced by invoking the highest potential of the mind and to approach an almost spiritual state of existence. The core value that Zeno considered among Socratic tenets of virtue was the element of wisdom. You can't just fall into the lap of wisdom. You have to work at it.

You work at attaining wisdom by focusing your mind on tangible and, more importantly, intangible dynamics that propel the visible and discernable tangible events. You do it by subjecting those focused observations to serious contemplation and reflection. That needs a focused mind, and a focused mind is achieved by quelling the chaos and embracing the silence.

The strategies laid out above should get you to that point.

Chapter 7 - The Layers of Contemplation

"Whatever this is that I am, it is flesh and a little spirit and an intelligence. Throw away your books; stop letting yourself be distracted. That is not allowed. Instead, as if you were dying right now, despite your flesh. A mess of blood, pieces of bone, a woven tangle of nerves, veins, arteries. Consider what the spirit is: air, and never the same air, but vomited out and gulped in again every instant. Finally, the intelligence. Think of it this way: You are an old man. Stop allowing your mind to be a slave, to be jerked about by selfish impulses, to kick against fate and the present, and to mistrust the future."

*— **Meditations, Emperor Marcus Aurelius Antoninus Augustus, 180AD***

A Stoic's ability to contemplate and reflect is like a wizard's wand. It is the seat of his strength and power. His wisdom and the virtues that flow from it are found in his ability to contemplate on matters and reflect on them deeply.

While you practice getting to your silent space, you will find that with each new session you will be able to hold that silence even longer than before. As the span of silence gets longer, you are better prepared for deeper contemplation.

You need this silence in the mind because there are strands of thoughts that can be so delicate that a disquieted mind could shatter the thought. Trying to contemplate with a chaotic mind is more frustrating than productive.

Ideally, you will contemplate in alternating fashion. Start with silence, and when the mind has focused, begin contemplation of the areas you wish to think about. If your mind starts to wander and dig up things that aren't related, let it go for a while and see where it takes you. If you feel that it is too far off the beaten path, then go back to a period of silence and come back to the thought again later.

When Stoics contemplate, they are looking for the nature of that which they are observing. Their contemplation is really a series of whys, how's, and so on. That is the basics of contemplation. You can only see the nature of hits with your mind, and that is what contemplation gives you.

If you don't do this, you will find that you don't have a grip on all the answers while you try to think about them. That's because your mind only stores a minimal amount in your conscious brain. When you are distracted, those distractions are taking up space.

The conscious part of the brain has limited space and limited power to process. The bulk of the matter exists in cognitive suspension in the subconscious part of the brain.

When you cogitate on an issue, you will find that you may be able to work on the issue at a conscious level before coming to a halt. This is because the conscious mind and powers of reasoning at this level can only go so far. To go any deeper and analyze better, the Stoic taps his subconscious processes.

To trigger their subconscious process, Stoics use the powers of silence. When one remains silent for ten minutes and keeps all thoughts and sounds at bay, it is easier for the subconscious mind to move answers to the conscious part of the brain.

When you silence your mind and contemplate a question, you will find that you now have additional answers that you didn't have earlier. This is the most important reason you practice silence even when you are not contemplating anything.

Contemplation

Contemplation is the way the mind digests the subject. This contrasts with observing, which is the way the senses capture the object.

The purpose of the earlier exercise of moving your focus to the sounds in order of descending volume is to train you among other things to be able to focus on what you choose. If you don't gain control over where your focus goes, you will always be at the mercy of external events and distractions.

The next level contemplation is to use reason, logic, and conscious effort to work out possibilities in your head. Until now you have only engaged in conscious processes in your head. One can do that for simple matters but will find it impossible to gain any real benefit in complex situations.

Reasoning and debating can get you part of the way to where you need to be to make a decision or to know the true path that you should follow, but it doesn't take you all the way.

Stoics, however, go one step further. The next stage of contemplation that Stoics engage in happens at a subconscious level. The conscious mind is ideally suited to make observations but not suited to decipher the nature of complex phenomenon.

One of the greatest warriors and generals of all time was the young king of Macedon in the early part of 300 BC. He eventually conquered the largest kingdom in the world at the time—the Persian Kingdom—and was crowned Alexander the Great. At the time of his battles, young Alexander was in his early to mid-twenties—rather young and rather successful without the benefit of mature thinking molded by experiences.

Within a short span of time after leaving Greece on his conquest of Asia, he was able to rule a large part of the known civilized world and a pretty sizeable area of uncivilized tribes to become one of the richest and most powerful men in history. The deciding battle in his victory over the Persians that set this path was fought in modern-day Kurdistan. If it sounds like any other battle in ancient times, it's not. The battle was decisively won, and it splintered the alliances of the Achaemenid Empire. What was amazing, however, was that the Achaemenid Empire came to the battle with a million soldiers. Alexander showed up with fewer than 50,000 men, a ratio of 1:20.

When the battle was done, Alexander had lost less than 1,000 men. His battle plans had been flawless, and his soldiers had executed them brilliantly. How does this relate to contemplation?

Alexander met with his generals the day before the battle and listened intently to their suggestions and plans. The odds, according to the generals, were overwhelmingly against them.

They had all told him that engaging the Persian army would be suicide. Spies had ridden out and scouted the size of the army and reported back with their count. The generals and captains were more than uncomfortable and predicted total loss if the battle proceeded.

Alexander, however, was undaunted. He told them to get ready, eat well, and prepare for the following morning. He then went into his tent and sat down alone. While his generals and soldiers stayed in camp, Alexander sat contemplating for hours in silence. Then he went to sleep.

The following morning the troops were supposed to move out early and enter the battlefield, but the generals had not seen any sign of Alexander. When General Parmenion couldn't find the king anywhere, he went to his tent and shouted many times for him until he finally emerged. The king had overslept.

Parmenion was surprised and asked him how he could sleep, much less oversleep, on the day of the most important battle of his life. In response, Alexander told him to relax and that the battle had already been won. What remained was that they just had to show up for the fight. Alexander had used the power of his mind to play the whole battle in his mind and already knew the outcome.

Historians and priests have long debated his divine inspiration on the eve of the battle. What had happened was that he had gone into a deep state of contemplation, and at the end of it he had found the nature of the event and his strategy and knew what to do.

When General Parmenion came to his tent that morning, Alexander briefed him, and it was carried out. They vanquished an army twenty times their size. That is the true power of contemplation, and it is what defines the power of the Stoic mind.

The main driver of efficiencies that Stoics are famous for is found in that subconscious area of their minds. That area holds the bulk of the processing power and thus the answers to many of their questions. This is part of the reason they never languish in indecision. Doing so is a common symptom of those who have competing perspectives, competing values, or competing desires tugging at them internally. When you straighten these things out, process them effectively, and align them, you find that clarity ensues.

Reflection vs. Contemplation

There is a simple difference between reflection and contemplation. You need to do both, but you need to be clear about the nature of each one. Reflection is the ability to replay the events from the past in your head and look at them individually and find common areas of concern. It is a teaching and self-learning tool. It is not easy for your conscious mind to understand why you do a lot of things, and it is not easy for you to understand some of your motivations for doing what you do. Reflection helps you to observe your own actions and trace a path back to the motivations that result in those actions.

Stoics are very efficient and effective people. They are efficient in the things they do and the issues they think about. They use all that is available to them, even the deeper abilities of the mind.

Stoics value this clarity, and it is the easiest path to identify the truth when it appears and appreciate it. Reflection and contemplation allow you to build yourself to a point that allows you to remain clear of distractions and aligned in purpose. If nothing else, these are the goals and objectives that you should aim for in your quest to understand Stoicism.

To draw the distinction between reflection and contemplation is to be able to see that while they cover most of the same areas you need both to be able to take advantage of the other.

You need reflection to be able to enhance your contemplation powers, and you need contemplation to be able to bring benefit to your reflection. When you fine-tune both of them, you find that the result is exponentially beneficial.

Chapter 8 - A Stoic's Meditation

Imagine a clear glass of water. If you were to place a drop of yellow pigment in it, imagine what would happen. That yellow dye would permeate and diffuse through the water. Even if you don't stir it or shake the glass, as time passed, the dye would diffuse gradually until it occupied the entire space of water. Would it jump out of the water and occupy the air above it? No. Its universe would be the confines of the water, and it would not be able to exit its universe.

Extending that same imagery, you can see that the form of that dye—that cloudy appearance of yellow permeating that water—is suspended in a medium. Without that medium, the dye would not manifest in that same way. That die owes its form to the medium that holds it.

In the same way, the mind, like that yellow pigment, is predicated on a medium. When you need to access the mind's higher level functions, you can't do it in the same way you involve conscious functions. You have to do it by accessing the silent part of your mind—the medium in which the mind floats.

The challenge most people have is to focus on that silence. Because the mind is active and its job is to throw up thoughts and concerns, you find that it is constantly making some sort of observation or alerting you to some possible thought. You have to extract yourself from paying attention to it when you need to, and then the mind will start to tune down.

Think of your total mind as an echo chamber except in this case it's perpetual, and you can stop it until you curtail at least one side of the equation.

Without going into the workings of the mind too deeply, imagine blasting an echo chamber with a sound. What would happen? The chamber will bounce the sound back at you. What if you put another echo chamber across from it? The sound would echo again. It does this a couple of times and then dies down as the energy in the sound wave diminishes much like the ripple in a bucket that bounces back and forth until the energy of the ripple diminishes. Then it goes back to being calm again. That only works when the original echo chamber is passive.

In the case of your mind, it is not passive. Your mind works on the principles of association. If you say one word, it will automatically (and almost magically) respond with another word, and that word will trigger another word, and that will trigger another. So if you were to play the word association game, you will see that the mind is an endless source of seemingly random thoughts or fragments of thoughts.

It is anything but random.

The Mind and Intangibility

The world is composed of two phenomena. The first is tangible—having, for example, shape, size, and mass. A shoe is an object, just like an apple or a car. These are tangible factors.

The second phenomenon is intangible. For instance, whether the car is moving or stationary are intangible qualities. A good way to think about it is to wonder if you can take a picture of it. If you can, it's tangible. If you have to resort to a video recording of it to show the changes it makes, then that is very likely intangible. In this case, movement and acceleration are all intangible properties. A larva's metamorphosis into a butterfly is intangible, but the butterfly and the larva are both tangible.

With respect to these kinds of tangible and intangible properties, it is the mind that can decipher them, which has to be done through contemplation. The brain creates memories of the result and stores it as part of the neural record. The mind is the only tool in a person's arsenal that can convert intangible phenomena into tangible representations in the form of neurons.

The mind has a stage that is built within it, and on that stage it places representations of the various experiences and objects it comes in contact with. Without that representation in the mind, the objects that appear in the physical reality will seem unreal to us. On the other hand, if we have something in our mind but it is missing in the real world, we tend to overlook it at times or feel uncomfortable.

Take, for instance, your home. You are completely familiar with it, and your mind has every detail of the physical space replicated and represented on this stage that it built in the mind.

When you enter this place, the mind is totally at ease with the surroundings because it's exactly as it should be. The observation the mind receives and the neurological imprint the brain has in store are identical. In fact, if the mind is not aware of an alteration in the physical world, it may even neglect to look at its surroundings carefully and might miss something that may have been moved.

Alternatively, think about the first time you went to a certain place. Do you recall the feeling you had in that strange place? It's a heightened state that will have you alert and observant. The more and more you visit that location after that, the more relaxed you start to feel, and you are no longer as alert or as observant as before.

In fact, you may even take things for granted after some time. You could even close your eyes and know exactly where everything is because of that neurological imprint of your environment.

The mind is not looking at your physical surroundings and making decisions directly. It is making decisions on that virtual stage built in your mind. That works for both tangible and intangible phenomena.

Here is one way you can visualize that. If you've played tennis, you would realize that the ball is too fast for the eye to catch and respond. In fact, your mind only anticipates its location based on what it sees your opponent doing and the kind of court you are playing on. It calculates from there and allows you to react. If it gets it right, then it reaffirms the calculation it uses. If it gets it wrong, then it updates the calculations. That's why the more you practice, the better you become.

How does meditation come into this?

It comes back to your physical mind. Remember that your memories are made of neurons, and each neuron is connected to other neurons by axons. Each neuron can have numerous connections—dozens, hundreds, or thousands. When you play the word association game, one word will trigger another because they have this connection between their respective neurons.

It turns out that these connections are not fixed. They can be altered, and the neurons can be moved around. This is called neuroplasticity, and it specifically refers to the alteration of the layout of the neurons and the ability of the brain to alter what neurons connect to, which, in turn, results in thinking patterns that can be altered.

If someone has a poor mind-set in that they constantly think of bad outcomes and they associate negatively, then anytime they hear a certain trigger word or phrase or are exposed to almost anything, it will fire up a range of neurons that are destructive in nature.

This comes down to a simple issue of just poor associative connections, and they can be altered by reconnecting the neurons through a process called neuroplasticity. Stoics in 300 BC didn't know anything about scientific neuroplasticity, but they did understand the power of reconditioning the mind to improve the decision-making process. That, in turn, improves outcomes.

That brings us back to perception, reflection, and contemplation. When you understand reflection and contemplation, you are forced to deal with issues with the same groups of neurons firing whenever you approach a certain issue—just as you may constantly be shouting the word "shoe" each time you play the word association game when someone else shouts "brown." Somehow in your neurological set the word "brown" is related to a brown shoe, so you respond by saying "shoe" when they say "brown."

You're not going to always pick "shoe" because on different days the choice of the responses may jump the neurons from one step to the next or down two steps or even ten steps. The universe of possible responses is fixed by what your neurons are connected to. It can be any number of responses, but those responses can only work if they are connected. If you have "cucumber" on a different set of neuron connection, the utterance of "brown" is never going to evoke your mind to respond with "cucumber."

Think of your different neuron sets as a multiverse of possible neuron bunches. It's easier to think of them in binary terms about whether or not each bunch is connected. In reality, it comes down to how many connections exist in the brain. All bunches are connected with at least one connection. If they are not connected, the probability of getting to that memory drops to exactly zero. If you want the simple explanation, then just think of them in the multiverse. The higher the number of connections emanating from a neuron, the greater the chance that that neuron will be invoked.

If you look at an MRI of a brain during its regular activity, you will see flashes of energy around areas of activity. These flashes seem random but are not. They gravitate in waves of associated neurons. When these neurons fire, they trigger the neurons they are connected to, which means that when you have an idea or are subjected to a specific event, you will always have the same associative thought that triggers in its wake.

The only way to change that is through cognitive conditioning and neuroplasticity. This is where meditation applies. When you meditate, the neurons are moved around and aligned in a more efficient arrangement. What you find is that one event triggers a different set of thoughts and responses than it did before the relocation of the neuron. The more you meditate, reflect, and contemplate, these neurons arrange themselves in a better formation, and you are destined to have better cognitive outcomes.

The Stoics during Zeno's time did not come close to knowing the neuroplasticity effects of meditation. What they did know was that there were positive effects from it. It altered the way they thought, and when the altered thinking sequence yielded better outcomes, the positive reinforcement solidified the change.

That is the whole idea of a Stoic's meditation.

Chapter 9 - Anger and Stoicism

"Keep this thought handy when you feel a fit of rage coming on—it isn't manly to be enraged. Rather, gentleness and civility are more human, and therefore manlier. A real man doesn't give way to anger and discontent, and such a person has strength, courage, and endurance—unlike the angry and complaining. The nearer a man comes to a calm mind, the closer he is to strength."

— Meditations, Emperor Marcus Aurelius Antoninus Augustus, 180AD

Stoics approach the topic of anger with the primary purpose of understanding its deeper roots and motivations. The eventual understanding of anger that results from this approach then leads to the ability to limit its force in the Stoic's thought pattern and annihilate its effects across other psychological and physiological areas.

Anger in whichever form, however intense, and under whatever condition is a distraction to rational thought and thus an obstacle to a Stoic's desired state of mind.

Anger is a term that applies to a wide range of states, ranging from mild irritation at the low end of the spectrum to a fly-off-the-handle rage that exists at the far end. The state of anger at any degree does not exist in a vacuum nor can it be spontaneously created or extinguished. However, it almost always seems to the person that endures it as though it comes from nowhere and leaves a swath of destruction in its path before suddenly disappearing. It's no wonder that Stoics call it a temporary state of madness.

Just as a hurricane that seemingly comes from nowhere wields destruction in its path and then vanishes after an inexplicable intervening event can be studied and understood so, too, can anger. It, too, seemingly swells from nowhere, destroys things in our path, and then quells after some intervening event be it time or our better angels. The similarities don't seem to end there.

Just as the hurricane has causes that we can't see with the naked eye, anger's causes are not easily detected by our consciousness, and that is why we think that it comes from nowhere. This fallacy is the main reason those with anger problems and those who only experience anger occasionally think they do not have the wherewithal to control anger.

Anger, in its original design, is about regulating the response to a particular situation a person is faced with, but anger is not a simple emotion. It is not just one faculty of the mind, such as fear or hunger. Anger is a complex state that is the amalgamation of various faculties in the mind.

By understanding the genesis of anger and seeing how a Stoic overcomes it, we draw benefit from two areas: (1) we can use the same strategies to our own bouts of anger, and (2) we are able to understand the mind-set, philosophy, and nature of a Stoic.

Stoics are nothing if they are not master observers. To be able to observe, they invoke more than their senses. The invoke their mind and the powers of reason, and when they do this they start to take notice of the genesis of anger and the similarities of the causes and reasons behind each path that leads a person to that point of rage, irritation, or even frustration.

Stoics see anger as the attribute of a weak mind, which is easily swayed and inherently unstable. Instability is marked by the ease at which it can transition from a stable state to a state of chaos. In essence, a weak mind is one that can be knocked of its perch with the gentlest of breezes.

When you interact with a Stoic, there is almost nothing you can say or do that will destabilize them. Not only have they mastered the ability to not get angry, but they have also gone a few steps further. They have mastered their own mind to the point that it is not easily knocked off its perch.

The reason why anger is a good place to observe a Stoic's ability is because it is the easiest to fall into, the hardest to spot, and the most vexing of complex emotions. Once you have an understanding of how a Stoic manages anger, you can apply the same approach to many of your other situations.

When discussing anger, there are three stages of interest:

- The first stage refers to the elements that trigger the anger. These triggers are generally external (but could be internal as well) to the person and their mind. It is the point at which the person begins the process of cascading toward irrational behavior (anger).

- The second refers to the path that you start to traverse once the trigger has been initiated. It could start with getting cut off at the checkout counter, then someone cuts you off at the light on the way home, then someone jumps ahead and takes your parking spot. It's just a series of events that individually would not have been so much of an issue except that the original trigger set you on a course toward anger. We know this well and often refer to someone "going postal."

- The final stage is the manner in which that anger is expressed.

Stoics break down the complexity of anger by looking at its manifestation and, more importantly, the triggers that become full blown. Anger does not surface in a vacuous environment. It always has a cause whether that cause is real or an emotional response to a perceived event.

This allows Stoics to gain power over anger because both aspects of that understanding, i.e., that it is an emotional response and based on perception, are within one's field of influence. Who among you can say that you can't control your perception? Or, who among you can say that you can't control your response? You can.

You can control your perception, or you can control how you respond to the situation that results from that perception if you just pay attention to the moment. This is the reason why being in the moment and staying grounded in present reality is a key Stoic requirement.

Typically, we only control the outward action of a response to things that happen to us. So when someone cuts us off at the checkout counter, the irritation wells up inside, but the outward action is one of calm. This is especially so when we have to force ourselves to hold back our responses.

Stoics find this inefficient. So much energy goes into creating the original response and then more energy to hold it back. Instead, Stoics learned that if they could just alter the way they perceive incoming stimuli and alter those from being triggers, then they would not have to expend the energy to hold themselves back.

The Distortion of Anger

Putting aside the effect of anger on those around the aggressor, there is the matter of anger distorting present and future perceptions. This is equally detrimental to the person getting angry and the person facing his wrath.

To the person in the midst of an outburst, there is a situation that persists from the time the trigger is released and extends for a long time after the anger and the event in which it existed has passed. This is because the moment the trigger has been released the percolating anger begins to disrupt the person's perception, and everything that happens after that point is tainted. This is the first element of anger that is unacceptable to the Stoic.

The problem with distorted perception is that the information stored in one's memory during the outburst is not filtered or adjusted for that anger. It is stored as is, and that memory that is encoded is encoded with the element of anger that does two things—both detrimental to future issues. The first is that it taints that particular matter that was in discussion, and second it reinforces the state of anger because it is now associated with that event. The more anger outbursts a person has, the easier it becomes to walk the path toward a full-blown incident.

This distorts reality for the person who experiences anger.

The second distortion happens within the victim's psyche. The person that anger is directed to gets an avalanche of negative energy, and whatever is being communicated to them is not making sense because the angry person is incoherent and unreasonable.

Anger distorts the present and sets up the foundation of a distorted future. Anger gets baked into the mind-set of individual situations. As such, when a similar situation is triggered in the future, it triggers the feelings that were aroused in the face of anger, and that is unpleasant, distracting, and counterproductive. Anger is negative reinforcement and may be a short-term solution, but it is catastrophic in the long term.

Not only do Stoics choose to temper anger, they also choose to stay away from those who practice anger.

Chapter 10 - Stoic Minimalism

"Contentment comes not so much from great wealth as from few wants"

— *Epictetus*

Some of the things that the ancient Stoic philosophers did may shock you if you were to read accounts of their daily practices, but you have to move past the obvious impressions and take a step into the minds of these men. Socrates himself had a home and aids to assist with his endeavors, but some philosophers who developed Stoicism, such as Crates, Diogenes (not a Stoic but contributed to it), and Zeno, chose to live on the street without any possessions or security.

Take Diogenes, for instance. As you've read, he lived in a used olive oil barrel on the outskirts of the Athenian marketplace and panhandled for food. His time was spent thinking of life and higher pursuits. Think of all the threads that entails. No home means no shelter, no place to put food, or keep it clean. No washroom facilities and no moments of privacy. The list of what you don't have when you don't have a home and live on the street is endless. Not many would be able to do that today.

Not having a home means you have no need to spend time maintaining it, no need to earn to pay for it, no need to worry about what is going to happen to it, and no need to spend time on all the things that go into it. All that time you don't spend on a home results in time that you can put toward reasoning, cogitating, and seeing clearly without fear, favor, or frustration.

However, since this is not a book on asceticism, we don't want to advocate the complete abolition of possession. However, we look at it to make a simple point that the more you take out the need for material goods, the higher levels of contemplation your mind can reach.

This was primarily the reason Crates, Diogenes, and the hardcore philosophers of that time sought that kind of mental state to raise their thinking. There are certain areas in India and Vietnam where certain sects of Hindus and

Buddhists spend days panhandling for food near the temple to alter their perspective. Even though they know that after a day or more they will return to the comfort of their home and the food in their kitchen, the panhandling experience alters their minds in a way that allows them to think at a level of clarity that you just can't achieve with creature comforts of the modern home.

All this is nowhere close to what we need to accomplish in our efforts to embrace or practice Stoic virtues. We do, however, need to move in that direction to a certain degree. To put it in context, take a look at the life of someone such as Warren Buffet. Taking his life as an example makes a lot of sense, especially when you see that he is the third wealthiest person in the world behind Jeff Bezos and Bill Gates.

He still lives in a mediocre house and drives a used car—the same used car he drives to the airport to pick up his good friend Bill Gates. He lives an earthly and wholesome life that is so far in the background that it doesn't bother or distract him. There are others like him. Take

Kristen Bell, who showed up at the Oscars wearing a dress that cost less than $50; or Leonardo DiCaprio, who drives a Toyota Prius. These are people who make millions a year and regardless of whether or not they give to charity, the point is that they do not allow the trappings of wealth to blunt their mind, tarnish their soul, or alter their other gifts—and for this they get better at what they do and increase the quality and quantity of what they contribute.

Stoicism takes that path to minimalizing distractions a step further. In the same way, we made the point that religion is like processed food and Stoic philosophy is like whole food. The point is that you need to take time to understand and feel the wisdom for yourself.

The cornerstone of Stoicism is wisdom, but to get that wisdom is not about how much you read. It's about how much you contemplate. When you take philosophies and use them as guidelines, they become dogma and pretty soon are indistinguishable from religions and laws that tell you what you can and can't do without ever knowing the reason why.

Take, for instance, this topic of Stoicism. To really understand and benefit from it, you should equip yourself with the knowledge that is available, but that is not the end of it. It can't be sufficient because what we read and hear can never communicate all that is required to reach a state of happiness and accomplishment. What we need is the contemplation that happens in the midst of acquiring this knowledge.

To put it simply, reading gives you knowledge. Experience gives you insight. Contemplation of that knowledge and insight gives you wisdom. To be able to get that wisdom, you can't be constantly distracted and aloof. That's where minimalism is important. People such as Diogenes shunned all possessions, including the materials that one needs to live on a day-to-day basis. He also gave up on accolades and matters of pride, such as adulation and the need for respect from others. In this respect, when he was called a dog because he was out roaming the streets almost naked and eating trash or what was given to him, he responds with glee, saying that a dog has a heightened sense of awareness, always living in the moment and not having the anxiety of what comes next.

In today's context, that kind of behavior is rather extreme and most likely inappropriate, but hearing the story in its raw form can do one of two things in you. It could either invoke a feeling of disgust and judgment, or it could cause you to stop and think about what Diogenes was trying to say and why so many people shun the world of material goods even if they have made a tremendous amount of money.

There are two points that are being presented: (1) the direct issue of distraction and (2) the importance of contemplation.

As for the first point, the richer you are, the greater the possibility of and propensity for distraction. That distraction is not just about what you can do with your wealth. It is also about how you see yourself and the fact that you think you have already made it. Stoicism sees the opportunity to be minimalist as a way to avoid factors that would otherwise cause you to spend time away from contemplating tangible and intangible events. To be able to understand the soul (the pneuma) of things, you have to see it with your mind and can't be distracted.

Today, it is not possible for you to live on the streets and contemplate the state of life or the pneuma of anything at the same time. It was all right for those men in Athens, where it didn't get too cold at night, or if it did there was always a way to get warm. But you can't do that in Buffalo, New York, in the middle of winter. Having a home today is a necessity to keep you protected from the elements.

The Aristotelian principle that eventually made its way into Stoic teachings was insistence that balance was more important than extremes, and many Stoic teachers in the Late Stoa did eventually realize that the extreme did detract from the objective more than they contributed.

That brings us back to the happy medium—the Aristotelian Golden Mean, which never officially made it into the writings of the Stoics, but they did eventually see its benefit. The Golden Mean does not advocate minimalism, but it does advocate balance between extremes.

How does the balance of extremes come about to being minimalist, since minimalism sounds like an extreme in and of itself? Minimalism is not an extreme situation. In fact, the moniker itself is misleading. Putting the notion of the name aside, lets associate the name to what it really is and not what it seems to indicate.

On the one hand, you have absolutely nothing. No clothes, no home, certainly no vehicles, and no prospect of a future meal or any kind of comfort—literally the life of a dog, as Diogenes relished in. That is the extreme end of the spectrum, and that is the life of an ascetic. On the other end, there is an absolute and indulgent luxury. Not only do you have everything you need for today, but you also have everything you need for three lifetimes—that's the quantitative dimension of excess.

Not only can your cell phone make a call, but it can also drive a car. Not only can your house give you safety from the elements, but it can also house an entire army. Forgive the exaggeration. The point is that luxury denotes a two-dimensional state. Not only do you have more than you need (quantitative) (e.g., the number of rooms in your house, but you also have it painted in gold (which has no practical purpose). That's qualitative.

Minimalism seeks to blunt both edges of that sword. It seeks to occupy the mental space where you don't need to subject yourself to an ascetic lifestyle, and you don't need the quantitative or qualitative aspects of excess. You straddle the middle.

It is rather tricky to find where the center of mass is in this equation. If you don't want to be naked like an ascetic and dress in golden threads like Midas, then what is the center of those extremes?

The answer is simple, which is the first point of minimalism. You have to contemplate. Getting a list of things that you should throw out or steps you should take to get yourself to be a minimalist is not the best way to be successful. Remember that Stoicism is not about following steps or completing lists. It is about contemplation. Only when you contemplate will you be able to find wisdom.

Once you get to that point, you should ask yourself if that is the minimalism that you envision, or are you now richer than you expected? The answer to that is pretty shocking for most people.

Once you shun the excess because those excesses are going to be more of a distraction, then what you find is a life that is uncomplicated and uncluttered. That reduction of clutter has many therapeutic effects, but that is not the reason you set a course on understanding minimalism. You chart this course to minimalism as a twofold exercise. The first is to mold your mind into contemplation, while the second is to understand the nature of contemplation.

Let's look at another example. They are not directly related to minimalism in the common sense of the word, but they are alerted to the way the human psyche approaches them and the faculties of the mind that are involved in both those areas.

For this, take a look at fasting. What do you suppose are the general reasons for fasting? The most common one is to lose weight or be healthy. When is that the rationale behind fasting? Someone who is in good health with an ideal weight (or even a little under the ideal weight) would not consider fasting, but fasting is not just about the food aspect of it. Fasting is about the resilience of the mind. To be able to stop something that is perceived to be imperative to survival makes the mind stronger. By fasting, you shift the power balance between the body's request and the mind's resolution.

This is the higher purpose of fasting. In the same way, there is a higher purpose for minimalism. When you contemplate the nature of being minimalist, you will first learn that you are merely getting yourself back to basics. Why buy a car that has twelve wheels when you can just as easily get to work in a car that has four (or even three)? Why take a car at all when you can get an Uber? But it goes beyond that as well, and when you peel back the next layer of minimalism, what you find is that the human mind is built to take things to the next level. That even applies to excesses. Today, you buy a car that unceremoniously takes you from Point A to

Point B. Tomorrow, you want that car to have a stereo in it; the day after you want it to be able to travel rocky terrain (even though you don't necessarily do that); the next day you want it to be able to have all kinds of gadgets and gizmos and consume a gallon of fuel for every 3 miles that you drive. We tend to snowball into excess. That's the human condition. That snowballing takes up tremendous energy, uses valuable time, and hits us in a spot that we don't even realize—pride. Suddenly, we want a bigger car just so we can show off to our neighbors who don't really care what car we drive.

Stoic minimalism is about taming the excesses so that we come back to a mind that is undistracted by all that is petty. As such, minimalism serves two important purposes: (1) to stop possible distractions and (2) to place the mind on a higher trajectory.

However, there is a catch to all this. If you follow a list of things to do and get rid of that gets you to be a minimalist, then you have lost the plot. Completing your current situation and where you need to be is part of the process. If you have a Humvee as your vehicle, an onlooker may say that's an excess and tell you that that is the first thing you need to get rid of to be able to get on the path to being a minimalist. However, what if that Humvee were a source of your work? Let's say you are a tour guide in the tropical forests and you use that Humvee for guided tours. That Humvee, to you, is not an excess. That is why you cannot look at a geode book and get rid of the things they ask you to get rid of.

Instead, you need to look at all the things you do possess and ask yourself what purpose they have in your life. The key is matching its purpose to your purpose. Just like the man with the Humvee. For him, it's not an excess, but that same Humvee would not be for you if you live right across from your workplace and just need to cross the road to get here.

Your track toward minimalism is most likely going to be one that is gradual. You must not shock the system, but you should build your strength as you walk the path. Remember that you are building your wisdom as you take on this exercise as much as you are shunning distraction.

Stoic minimalism has a higher purpose. It is there to get you to contemplate your path and remove the layers of distraction that are around you. In time you will see that minimalism is not just applicable to tangible objects but also to intangible phenomena. For instance, you will start to realize that you do not need the adulation of your fellow man because you owe your pleasure to something of a higher order.

The heart of a Stoic is driven by his sense of duty first and foremost. His duty is not about serving any one man or group of people. This is a common misconception. You are not a slave to anyone, but neither are you lord over anyone either. You have a skill and intellect that is unique to you, and your sense of duty is to use that skill and intellect for the good of all those around you in any way you can. It is not to be proud of your ability but to be humble in its execution. It is not to receive praise for your ability but to know that you have to keep your head down and do more.

When Nathan Hale was captured in New York and executed, he said, "I only regret that I have but one life to give." It is not clear if he was Stoic, but that doesn't matter. No one is baptized into Stoicism or excommunicated from it. You are Stoic by the life you live, and Nathan Hale's mind-set after being caught by British troops indicates that he lived a life of duty for that in which he strongly believed—American independence.

Minimalism allows you to focus on the duty that you are uniquely designed to perform. If that sounds like a hint of socialism or communism since the greater good is achieved by contributing to others, then there is a missing facet in the understanding of one's presence in life. Duty is about what you give to everyone without expecting any measure of return except knowing that you have done what you were designed to do. In other words, you have served your purpose.

It so happens, however, that many modern-day Stoics have become very wealthy by doing their duty and contributing to society. In many cases, that works for a long time because they do not get distracted by the wealth; instead, they keep their heads down, shop at Target, and drive Toyotas.

To wrap up let's tie together some of the issues and the general themes in Stoicism so that you can bring minimalism into your life without wasting it on misunderstanding its power. If you blindly follow a to-do list and build a list of things that you have in your home to get rid of, you will waste the entire benefit of the exercise. You will look at the moment you gave all your things away and feel totally empty.

Instead, what you should do is look at each object in your possession and understand why you have it. The questions should be specific. If you are asking why you own a car, you should ask yourself why you own that specific car. Was there something lesser that you could have gotten? The answers have to be frank, honest, and consistent. Saying that you bought the car because you like it won't pass muster.

When you look at each object in your possession and pose these probing questions repeatedly and relentlessly, what you will inadvertently find is your own weaknesses and your own inconsistencies. If you have five coffee mugs that you use on a rotating basis, ask yourself why you have five. Why isn't one mug able to do the job?

When you whittle everything away by asking why you own something, you will find that you accumulate things that you don't need because you are trying to solve a deeper problem by association. If you have a lack of self-confidence, you may buy a bigger car regardless of how much debt you have to incur to do it. That car represents a need to compensate.

So, when you shine a light on it, you find insight into yourself. That insight is what makes the process toward minimalism so important and valuable. Don't trade that in for a meaningless list that tells you that you need to get rid of your car and take the bus, downsize your home and get an apartment, and wear cheaper clothes. You have to decide what is right for you—what you need to get rid of and why. That's the point of Stoic minimalism. It's the process, the intangible of the exercise—the so-called pneuma.

Until you do, getting rid of the object does you no good whatsoever.

Contemplation leading to minimalism is like teaching a child to not be afraid of the dark. You have to start with rationalizing the contents of the dark room and then go around the room and provide evidence that there is nothing under the bed or in the closet and then turn the lights off while holding their hands to assure them. At this point, you can introduce them to the concept of imagination. Just as the imaginative forces are confused with real observation in children, adults associate tangible things with intangible benefits that don't exist. For instance, how exactly does a Mercedes confer status in the mind of a stranger? What exactly are you hoping to get when you buy a BMW? When you buy a car, are you looking to get from A to B, or are you looking for pleasure?

Gradually, you start to see that it is all in your mind and that you don't need that Mercedes or BMW to make you happy. That's the real purpose of the contemplative process in Stoic minimalism. If you just decide, on a whim, after reading this or any other book to get rid of all that you have, it would have no benefit.

The train of thought in any reasoning process to adopt Stoic virtues is so that you find true and lasting happiness. However, the last thing you want to do in that process is to use a step-by-step guide to do it. Such guides are fine for making chocolate chip cookies but not for finding lifelong happiness.

Chapter 11 - Righteousness

"To righteousness, in speaking the truth freely,
and without ambiguity; and in doing all things
justly and discreetly. Now in this good course,
let not other men's either wickedness, or
opinion, or voice hinder thee: no, nor the sense
of this thy pampered mass of flesh: for let that
which suffers, look to itself."

— **Meditations, Emperor Marcus Aurelius**
Antoninus Augustus, 180AD

Speaking the truth does not stop at not telling lies. It is an entire array of conduct that exists on a plane. Being technical, yet misleading is not righteous. Being truthful but incomplete is not being righteous. And, being ambiguous for the purpose of evading the real question, yet not wanting to seem evasive is not righteous.

Being righteous is more than just the words we use or the quality of the representations we make. The words mean nothing if the actions that preceded them or followed them are flawed.

It comes back to the issue of wisdom. You have to have the wisdom to know when doing something is wrong. At the core of all this is that we are striving for happiness, and we gain the ultimate happiness by doing our duty.

Doing our duty to the world at large means we have to be virtuous in our conduct and honest in our thoughts, words, and deeds. Stoics, by advocating that happiness comes from virtue, automatically and explicitly embrace righteousness as well and find that it is a necessary condition to be able to be dutiful and thus gain happiness.

The problem that we so often face in the reality, however, is that our ambition, goals, and objectives come at odds to being dutiful, and it becomes more about selfishness and self-serving benefits at the expense of those to whom we owe our duty. When this happens, righteousness experiences fracture.

It has come to the point that we are willing to indulge in unrighteous acts and yet speak with honey potions on our lips to be able to cover the action that we think is warranted. We often act and then find that our actions deserve covering, and then we engage in lies and half-truths. These are all consequential issues and not the root of the matter.

The seed of destruction is planted when we slip from doing our duty and instead focus on serving our own needs and excesses. How do we know we are on that slippery slope? The only way to know is to ponder each action before it is executed. Knowing what you are doing is the key to being aware of your actions.

If you do not know the consequences of your action, then it is only right that you postpone that action until you have had time to evaluate and contemplate it. If you use all the faculties of your mind in the contemplation of your action(s) and find that it is righteous, then you should proceed to do it. If you execute what you can honestly say was a righteous action but it turns out to be detrimental, then you have to take responsibility for it, learn from it, and move on without regret. That is the method of a Stoic.

There are two veins to this happiness and thus to this matter on righteousness. In Stoic material, you find that happiness has a specific meaning. It is not being happy because you won the lottery; it is not being happy because your children got into an Ivy League institution. These are random events of joy and satisfaction, not happiness. Happiness is something more profound in Stoic philosophy. While this may all just seem like semantics if you practice the kind of happiness that Stoicism is advocating, you will see it reverberate across all the areas of your existence.

Stoic happiness is comprehensive and doesn't stop at being in harmony with the tangible world. It is about living in harmony with the intangible as well. Think back to our discussion about intangible and tangible aspects of all things.

Remember what the Stoics mean when it comes to nature. We saw in an earlier chapter that everything has its nature. We saw that we have the spirit of things or the pneuma. We also saw that there are tangible and intangible issues, and being one with nature means that you understand the object and the nature of things.

In other words, you have to observe it and absorb it. You can see with your eyes, but you have to observe with your mind. When you do that, you start to understand the nature of things.

It is worth pointing out that the nature we are talking about is not just limited to the trees and bugs that inhabit this planet or the stars and the cosmic bodies that share this universe with us. It is about how all things behave, and that includes how the mind works in the absence of virtue and how consequences affect lives down the road based on the original action.

Righteousness requires that one reflect and contemplate the reason for righteousness. Stoicism can't be understood by a how-to article or a cookbook-type approach. Every step of Stoicism needs to be looked at from scratch and taken into consideration and molded to fit each individual's life and situation.

The question then becomes: How does that reflect on the topic of righteousness? The word itself can mean different things to different people. Modern vernacular assigns a slightly different connotation to it, and classical translators who took the original meaning from the Greeks meant something else. Even this book has defined it for you, but you need to sit down and understand what it means to you by yourself.

To reflect on and contemplate righteousness requires that you trace back a given event in your life. Let's take, for instance, being stopped for DUI. It's not bad luck. If you take the sequence of events that got you to this point, you will start to understand righteousness.

You were stopped because you were driving erratically, or it was a random stop. The event that got you stopped is not the problem. If you were not legally drunk, the stop would have been uneventful. You were driving intoxicated because you were drinking. That in itself could be a problem because you should know ahead of time that if you are going to be drinking you shouldn't be driving and vice versa.

If you take it back one step and ask yourself why you didn't think of things that way, you may find that you felt your desires or habits more important to fulfill than taking the risk with your life or breaking the law.

The key to back-tracing is to look back on the event and see where the root of that chain of events lies. In this case, it could go all the way back to the habit of drinking, or it could go all the way back to driving. If you look hard enough, you may decide to stop drinking or stop driving and get on the rideshare bandwagon. Both of which would be righteous in this case.

The key to contemplating righteousness is to not stop at reflecting on the event immediately preceding an unfortunate consequence but to throw back all the way to the genesis of the train of events. If you go back to the root of that chain of events, you may even realize that it has other possible consequences as well.

This hypothetical assumes that you contemplate righteousness in the wake of a problem. So, what about other times when something has not caused deep consequence? What if it is still lurking and waiting to rear its head?

This is when contemplation of all your actions, over time, comes in. If you look at all the things in your life and trace them back to the genesis act or thought process, then what you will find is the ability to define a set of righteous acts and thoughts.

You don't have to think about these in moral or immoral terms when you get started. Morality is a very different train of thought than righteousness. At this point in the book and in the shadow of Stoicism, we are not looking at right and wrong, moral or immoral. We are looking at the consequences of your life based on an action. The previous example had a little bit about legislation (DUI) mixed in, but that is not the focal point of the example. Do not mix up laws with righteousness. There are unrighteous laws, as Gandhi used to say. Righteousness has to do with nature and doing right by it. In return, you will find the peace and happiness that will elude you elsewhere.

One of the most common elements of righteousness is the concept of telling the truth. There are various benefits to this downstream.

The first is that telling the truth all the time gives you the peace of mind you need so that you do not have to keep track of the lies you tell.

More importantly, telling lies has un upstream complication, meaning that it can gravitate up to matters that precede the lie.

Let's look at this a little closer so as to not confuse the matter. If you lie and get away with it, your mind learns a new skill. It learns the art of getting away with lies. That's not always a good thing. It may have short-term benefits, but the long term is never good. Here is where the upstream issue comes in. If you start getting to the point that you can lie well, you will be inclined to do things that are not good because you know that you can lie about it later.

So, in essence, the ability to lie erodes your hesitancy to do things that go against the nature of things. If you steal someone's money and lie about it and get away with it, it will embolden you to steal again.

There are two kinds of truth-telling that you should be concerned with. The first is about telling the truth about things within your own gravity. If you did something wrong, you should own up to it. That way, you wouldn't have to lie about it, and, in the future, you wouldn't be emboldened to do more wrong acts.

Telling the truth works upstream and downstream. Stoics realize this from the very beginning and are not accustomed to lying or living a lie. There is a distinction in those two conditions. Telling a lie is the part where you speak falsely, but living a lie is when you live under the consequences of maintaining that lie, and that in many cases is significantly worse. Stoicism speaks furiously against this kind of life.

When Cato the Younger battled Caesar, he did so to protect Rome from possible tyranny. He had seen Caesar's ambition and had determined to block any attempt to slow-walk his beloved country into the hands of a dictator. He did it out of a sense of duty toward a greater purpose, and that signifies his adherence to the core of Stoicism. When his armies lost the attempt to check Caesar's army, Cato was certain that

Caesar would have him killed. But Caesar didn't have him killed but instead pardoned his rebellion. If he accepted that pardon, it would have meant that Cato would have to live a lie for the rest of his life. He knew that he would be forced to swear allegiance to Caesar—an allegiance that would be a lie. Instead of succumbing to that position, he committed suicide. That's how much living in truth meant to Stoics. Of course, today, it would be looked upon as ridiculous, but no one is asking us to do that right now, and most of us are not in that kind of position. But it is still wise to measure the weight of truth with Cato's example and see the relative importance it should have in our daily life.

Righteousness doesn't stop at just telling the truth. Righteousness blankets the existence of the Stoic with a sense of an all-pervading shield. It blankets the Stoic from reproach, it protects him from intimidation, it gives him the gravity of the righteous, and it imbues confidence because when he is righteous, he becomes imperturbable.

That shield is the ultimate state of strength. It can't be stolen, beaten, or incarcerated.

Chapter 12 - A Stoic's Individuality

"I have often wondered how it should come to pass, that every man loving himself best, should more regard other men's opinions concerning himself than his own."

— Meditations, Emperor Marcus Aurelius Antoninus Augustus, 180AD

There is a long-standing debate on whether Stoicism promotes individualism or collectivism. The debate is moot because the issue was actually settled more than two thousand years ago, but it is not hard to see why it is still misunderstood today.

On one side of the coin, much of the philosophy and ideology of the Stoic is based on improving the self and increasing one's awareness and one's righteousness. The four virtues of Stoicism—wisdom, justice, courage, and temperance—are all decidedly matters that are for the individual to handle within himself.

Some even go so far as to claim that Stoics should evangelize and force others to take on the righteous path of a Stoic. But this is wrong. There is no evangelization in Stoicism, just as you cannot learn to be Stoic from a how-to book. Evangelizing doesn't work in Stoicism because Stoicism is an experience and not a membership. Stoicism comes from inside after much contemplation, reflection, and meditation. It doesn't come after being lectured. If you have the opportunity to observe a Stoic, you will be able to learn more by what you see him do than by what you hear him say. That makes evangelizing impossible.

Then there is the other side of the coin. The sense of duty that we have looked at repeatedly thus far has a strange reflection of collectivism. This is probably why the debate is not a settled issue in some circles. To the untrained eye, there seems to be shades of individualism in some corners of Stoic thought, and there seems to be shades of collectivism in others.

The best way to look at this is a proverb that is told in Buddhist ashrams in the East. It fits the situation at hand perfectly:

Some time ago there was a father and daughter team of acrobats in a Chinese circus. The father would hoist the daughter on his shoulders, while she would balance herself on him and spin plates at the end of a stick. If either lost their footing, both would tumble onto each other to a catastrophic end. The father, worried about his daughter, kept telling her to be careful. His concern, while being a distraction to her, reduced his focus. After each act, she would tell him to not worry about her, and his response was that he was just doing his duty to look after her. In his mind, he was to look after her, and she was to look after him.

To this, she replied, "That is not the best way, father. If you worry about me and I worry about you, we will both make mistakes, and both of us will fall. But if I focus fully on what I have to do, and you focus fully on what you have to do, we will both turn out all right."

If both practiced individualism, their duty to each other would be fulfilled.

In the same vein as that parable, Stoics are arduous in their focus on what they do as individuals while knowing in the back of their mind that when they do that the whole would work out better.

Thus, the question comes back to whether Stoics are individualists or collectivists. At this point, the answer should be clear. We are both. We stand with the notion that we have the duty to serve, but we are not our brother's keeper.

To serve, in duty, we know that we have to have the wisdom to be able to provide justice, courage, and temperance. In turn, to have wisdom, we have to keep our eye and mind on the world around us and sharpen our minds. That is why the Stoics were the ones behind grammar and thought that it was paramount in the observation and dissemination of information and data.

That brings us back to individuality.

The pursuit of individuality is just as important as the attainment and practice of individuality. Individuality dovetails into a number of other areas in a person's life. When you think about standing up as an individual, you are looking at how to make your life your own and not following the opinions and judgment of others. Stoics don't care what others think of them. The extreme of this you could see in Diogenes (although he wasn't a Stoic; he was a Cynic). The strain of the Cynic school of thought that made it into the initial thoughts of Zeno and the subsequent foundations of Stoicism is that a person's character is strongest when they have no need to hold on to the expectations of others.

Individualism in Stoics is not about being alone or being isolated. It is about the strength of being independent and the strength to not be swayed by what others think. You can't live your life by poll numbers.

The stature of individuality is clasped by two polar requirements. On one side is the requirement of strength. Strength, in this sense, is not the muscles one flexes but the strength of righteousness. On the other side is the requirement of humility or the total lack of arrogance. It is easy to slip into arrogant states when pursuing the stature of individuality. While it is common to speak against that arrogance, it is not as common as finding the best way to go about it.

Practicing Stoics tend to deal with arrogance and promote humility within themselves by striking a balance between talking and listening. Shakespeare writes in Hamlet, "give every man thy ear, but few thy voice." It is the ultimate memory aid in thinking what a Stoic would do when confronted with the opportunity to be arrogant about not listening to another's opinion. Listening, just like seeing, is not something that you do with your senses but with your mind. Merely seeing with your eyes and hearing with your ears is not the way to go about "giving every man their ear."

Merely listening to their words will get you nowhere and will only waste your time. Listening with your mind, however, will give you insight into a number of things that you can't predict before you hear what someone else has to say.

That practiced gradually turns to a state where they know that much of what a person has to say may be irrelevant to the life of the Stoic in question, but, nonetheless, somewhere in the haystack, he may find the proverbial needle, and that is worth the effort. That renders the Stoics humble or at least be able to stand without arrogance.

Marcus Aurelius wrote in his journal, which was posthumously published under the title *Meditations*, that when one arises in the morning he or she should remind themselves that the day would be filled with all kinds of people coming up with all kinds of issues and problems, saying all kinds of things, and making all kinds of criticisms.

The goal of the Stoic is to not allow any of it to penetrate the shield of righteousness, yet patiently listen to what they have to say, and in the event there is something worthy in it, to add it to their own repertoire of knowledge so that they may tread forward enriched and enlightened.

Imagine for a moment if Zeno of Citium decided to walk away from a rambling man who claimed to speak of things previously unheard of. If Zeno didn't stop to listen to them, he wouldn't have had the opportunity to meet with Crates of Thebes, who taught him about the Cynic school of thought, and that sparked Zeno's thought process.

So now you have two sides of the individuality coin. On one side is the strength you need to stand on your own principles, thoughts, and actions. On the other side, you have the humility to be able to give someone your mind's ear.

Once that is done, the Stoic still has one more element in his armor that comes into play. It is the armor of contemplation and reflection. However strange or inane a person's position, if you look at it in its entirety, or if you look at it with your mind and understand what he or she is purporting, you will find that it makes sense on some level, and it will make sense to you. In other words, there will be something that you can benefit from it when you subject it to your mind.

Rene Descartes, the French philosopher, who was also a student of Stoic teachings, extends this individuality when he teaches the way one should hold another's words. He advocates listening to them and suspending your own beliefs and ideas even to the point of suspending your own reality while you listen clearly to what this other person has to say. Then while you have suspended your own view on the matter, investigate this new piece of information with fresh and unbiased eyes. When you are done, you have one of three courses of action to take. You can replace your belief and ideals with what you just learned. Or, you can reject the new idea but realize that there are those who still see this issue in a certain way. Or, finally, you can look at some of the issues that were in the idea, and some of the foundation of it could be used by you in your thinking.

There is nothing that anyone can say that has zero benefits to you if you listen and think carefully. A Stoic knows this. If you speak to a

Stoic, you can be sure that he will listen to all that you have to say, process it, and respond without ego and bluster no matter how opposed to the idea he may be.

Chapter 13 - Death & Stoicism

"How ridiculous and strange is he, that wonders at anything that happens in this life in the ordinary course of nature!"

— ***Meditations, Emperor Marcus Aurelius Antoninus Augustus, 180AD***

We end this book with a topic that is taboo in most conversations—one that concerns one's own mortality. Human beings, while they are hardwired to protect themselves and have the fear of death as a feature of their minds, are subjected to consequential and sometimes negative ripple effects from it.

The pleasures of life, the heartache of parting from loved ones, the thought of the ache in the life of those loved ones, not to mention the inherent fear of the unknown state, are all powerful reasons to fear physical death.

Stoics see death very differently from most philosophes in the East and West and differently from many of the major religions practiced today. To put it unceremoniously, Stoics see death as a natural extension of life. Because it is a natural extension of life, death, in itself, has zero impact on what a Stoic says and does.

In that same vein, Stoics see their responsibility to remain alive for as long as naturally possible as part of their duty so that they can be of service for the longest amount of time possible.

In Stoicism, there are two kinds of death. One is physical death, which is death that comes when the mind and body are no longer able to show signs of any life. The second is when the person's use to his fellow man around him has ceased. Remember again that a Stoic's life is in duty to the world at large. Total incapacitation to a Stoic is tantamount to death.

That incapacity could come as mental incapacity or physical incapacity, but in many cases, it even comes as intellectual incapacity or the incapacity to execute one's principles. Take the deaths of Cato the Younger and Brutus the Younger as an example.

That then begs the question. Does it mean that once a person is no longer able to perform his duty he is better off dead? Yes. But a person who is alive can find many ways to do a duty to the rest of his brethren; he just has to find it.

On the other hand, what about one's desire to keep one's self healthy and alive? Is that the wrong thing for a Stoic to do? No. It is the Stoic's duty to remain alive for as long as he can and to keep himself as healthy as he can so that he may be of service for as long as possible to as many as possible.

There is a lot of writing that weighs and discusses this topic in Stoic philosophy. Listing each one is beyond the scope of this book, especially when we can easily surmise the point that it all boils down to.

It comes back to the prospect of death being a powerful force in our life. Imagine if you were to live forever. Would you be motivated to do anything? It's like getting to a vacation destination and saying that you are going to live there indefinitely. Would you rush out of the hotel room as soon as you check in so that you can catch the sights on your first day there? No, you'd take your time.

It is the same with life. The idea that you are going to be here indefinitely would cause you to take it easy with things and not try to be all you can be or do all you could do. The knowledge of a finite present in this realm of living should make you want to spend more time absorbing all this level of consciousness allows.

Stoics realize that death is the greatest teacher and the greatest tool a person has if they are willing to contemplate it forward. When you fear death, have you asked yourself as a Stoic does, what is it that you fear? All questions that come in the wake of that question have a different flavor in their answer.

What do people who fear death actually fear? Is it pain? It can't be because there is no pain upon death, which by its very definition renders the senses nonexistent and thus the inability to feel pain. So, what is it to you? As a neophyte, you have to contemplate death to a degree that you are able to see it or what it is. If you are just starting out in Stoicism, this is a good place to start.

As a sidebar, to stress the level of importance that is inherent in the need for you to contemplate your own mortality, let us do a thought experiment. Imagine the color yellow. Now imagine having to explain that color using words alone to a person who has been blind all his life. How would you do it?

You wouldn't be able to get very far. Something similar happens in our quest to explain death in the context of living. We use the concept of beginning and end to denote points in a timeline, but to say that it is the end is not accurate. Stoics see it as a change in tangible circumstances because the pneuma is still intact. In death, the tangible ceases, but the intangible remains.

Language and conversations have limitations that preclude the communication of certain kinds of information. The only way to approach that information would be to contemplate it and/or to experience it. In the same way, the topic of death is not something that can be described but is something that can be contemplated.

It is natural to fear death. We naturally fear the unknown. All Stoics start in the same way as those outside the congregation of this philosophy. The difference is that Stoics start to weigh the matter by looking at that duty as the reason for them to maintain their life to the greatest extent possible but not an inch further. By focusing on duty and not death, they no longer fear it.

If fear overly animates our thoughts about something that is inevitable but not in the moment, then that fear has done more to harm than protect us. The fear of death when there is no logical and discernable reason or danger is not productive, and this is a distraction to the effective contemplation of all things.

To take up the life of a Stoic, contemplating death before you contemplate the other matters that have been discussed in this book will give you the necessary tools to extend all the other teachings, principles, and ideas that Stoicism has to offer.

Putting your life in order is wise so that it reduces your subconscious concerns that there are things that you have to fulfill but have not yet done. What one may fear is not fear of the unknown on the other side of death but rather the projected fear of not fulfilling one's duties on this side of death.

If that is the case, one has to focus on the fact that there is no time to waste, no time for idle chatter, no frivolous pleasures of the flesh, and certainly no time to be inefficient. These are all the things that you have to put in order posthaste.

Conclusion

The best way to get to know something is to dive straight into it, make mistakes, have misunderstandings, seek advice, and then spend the bulk of your time contemplating it and integrating it with one's own life experiences.

The conversation about Stoic virtues that is facing its renaissance in our lifetime has become vibrant over the last decade and more so in the last three years. Whether that indicates that the pendulum of human consciousness has swung from its apex in religious belief and disappointment or that we are just looking for answers in a world that has so many challenges is a contemplative proposition.

During this period of Stoic renaissance, it is worth our while to understand the genesis and the circumstances that existed in that time and the trajectory of events before Zeno landed in Athens. The point was that man has been looking to find his divinity. Whether it was placing his time in pursuing sanctioned religion from Christianity to Islam or unsanctioned beliefs from paganism to witchcraft, man has been on a quest to place meaning to life that goes from cradle to grave.

Therein lies the problem. He has limited his quest to between two distinct points in the journey—the day he was born and the day he will die.

Most teachings have failed to answer the question that percolates deep within when they only seem to intimate a limited purpose and a limited scope of life, but Stoics in their collective methods and plain pursuit of wisdom have opened a way for us to stretch our lives beyond the bookends of physical birth and physical death.

Life is more than that. It is not a drop in time. It is a continuum that extends from the point of the universe's creation and will continue while we evolve into higher and better forms of consciousness. There is no end to this just as your day doesn't end just because you turn in for the night.

Stoicism is not a set of rules and dogmas. In fact, it is not a fixed set of instructions for the way you should live your life. It is a compendium of thoughts and experiences that you can use. You do not need to be certified or experience a ritual to be inducted as a Stoic; in fact, you may already be one just by the way you conduct your life.

Gandhi was not a Stoic by admission, but his life and pursuit of duty and righteousness provide clear evidence of a life steeped in Stoic values. His wisdom and sense of justice for all applied with unshakeable courage and devout temperance at all times speaks volumes about what it is like to live a Stoic life.

The question remains, however, if happiness in the way it is defined in Stoic circles is something that resonates within you when you hear about it. If it does, then the path through Stoic values would be something that you can benefit from, and it will not detract from whatever religious beliefs that you may already have. In fact, it may give you the perspective you need to extract better value from it.

If, however, you don't see the point of Stoicism, then you should ask yourself which area of Stoic virtue is not vibrating with your inherent frequency. There is nothing wrong with not wanting to be Stoic, but not jiving with it is an opportunity for self-learning and getting to know yourself. At the very least, this book should place you on a path that will result in learning about who you are, what you are made of, and how that would turn out for you in the future.

When we look at life and compare it with the symphony, we see that the best way for all the parts to work is for each to follow its own purpose—just like the symphony and the father and daughter acrobats in the parable. To make sure the collective works, Stoics need to be highly individualistic, which requires focusing on improving the tangible and intangible aspects of one's existence.

Your desire to know about Stoicism may just be simple curiosity, or it may be the deep desire to fulfill the potential that is locked up inside you. Stoic practice is one of the most effective ways and efficient means to unlock the potential of the human mind and unleash the power of the soul.

Stoicism – Purpose and Perspectives

Ancient Wisdom for Modern Happiness

Stoicism – Purpose and Perspectives

Ancient Wisdom for Modern Happiness

How to Practice Stoicism in Your Daily Life

Kyle Faber

Stoicism – Purpose and Perspectives

Published by CAC Publishing LLC
ISBN: 978-1-950010-41-7 paperback
ISBN: 978-1-950010-40-0 eBook

Introduction

Stoicism has many levels just as there are many levels in almost everything one ventures into and seeks to understand. Whether it is chess or meditation, one typically begins as a novice and spends a lifetime pursuing iterations of progressively higher goals with increasingly complex concepts.

Just as a craftsman develops the touch of his hands, a runner develops the legerity of his legs, and a weight lifter develops the power of his arms, the Stoic is concerned with the development of his mental faculties.

The Stoic's mental faculties are distinct from practitioners of other schools of thought. Different schools of thought have different purposes and thus attract different personality types. The Stoic school of thought is open to anyone who is willing to endeavor and apply the necessary industry. The wise Stoic masters of two millennia ago were well beyond their generation, as they understood the neuroplasticity of the brain and the mind that is built upon it.

We are all born with a brain, but we are required to build our mind. One is endowed, while the other is endeavored. For the Stoic, he was not baptized at birth or coerced to become a Stoic. If he should decide to stop practicing the philosophy, he will not be ostracized or stoned for apostasy. Stoicism is not a religion, a cult, or a practice. It is a philosophy most concerned with the search for truth—whatever that truth may be. To be able to discern that truth, the tool that is needed is the mind. That tool needs to be sharp, powerful, and above all observant.

The human mind is built in such a way to accept and assimilate information. In its venture to do so, it values concentrated observation, contemplation, reflection, penetrating thought, and questions. In its industry to do so, it values silence. Without silence, the Stoic's perpetual state, the mind of the Stoic is not going to be effective or efficient to tackle the task.

Information and data are meaningless without the mind's participation. It's like baking a loaf of bread. The individual ingredients won't come together on their own. The baker needs to have a framework of what ingredients he should use and in what order he should use them. Once he is finished, he has to let nature take its course and allow the bread to rise before he bakes it and lets the oven take over. The mind needs to observe the data and information and then apply its faculties to understand it and make the information meaningful.

Just as the flavor of bread is individual in the hands of each maker, so, too, is the wisdom of the Stoic. His Stoic experience and his Stoic character, while based on the common elements of practice, will undoubtedly carry his particular brand. The worst thing one could do is hope to emulate every aspect of another Stoic's character and perspective.

To the novice, the vast sea of material, from books to pamphlets and journals to letters, may seem daunting and overwhelming, but one must remember that the fruits of Stoicism come from inside each novice, not from the information and the teacher outside. Within each novice is a complex web of confusion, knowledge, insight, and misconceptions that a person needs to organize within him and rearrange until it makes sense.

It may only seem complex at first, but the mind and the spirit will soon be able to grasp the simplicity of the truth because it is the soul's natural state to be silent, pensive, and at peace. The truth that the Stoic eventually discerns is in itself not difficult or arduous to approach. It is the misconception that we can't seem to let go of that obscures the data while clogging up the bandwidth. As such, one of the first steps the Stoic must take is to make it a habit to question his motives, analyze his assumptions, and test the consistency of the facts. Only then will he be able to approach and appreciate the truth.

That's a long to-do list. It is something the mind is totally capable of doing, but it does take a lot of brain power, especially when the faculties of the mind and the machinery of the brain are tied up with distractions. These distractions are a waste of resources—energy and time—which is why Stoics naturally gravitate toward silence inside and out.

In fact, it is almost the definition of a person who is silent, pensive, and at peace to be referred to as being stoic in nature.

The core of Stoicism is built with silence. For one to be able to embrace, appreciate, and benefit from it, one has to first condition the mind to accept the lip's silence. The rule is simple: If it is not absolutely necessary, it does not need to be uttered. The same applies to the mind. If the thought is absolutely not needed, it is not meant to be debated and thus should be passed over in favor of silence.

Silence is a widespread state that goes beyond the cessation of sound from the lips or the sounds that reach us through the auditory faculties. Sound also refers to the chaos of the unrestrained mind, the chatter of random thoughts, and anything that we process through the auditory cortex. Every sound that is received or generated by the mind stresses the resources of the mind and results in a correspondingly reduced direction of the mind to more fruitful endeavors.

It may be surprising to learn as one embarks on a self-restrained course of silence that it is easier to restrain the lips' chatter than to harness the mind's babble, but the latter is almost as important as, if not more than, the former for embracing silence. A silent mind can easily convince the lips to follow suit, but silent lips will not have such luck with the mind if the mind is in a state of undisciplined habit.

The path to silence is found with practice, which means improvement and elevation. That is a matter of human nature. Even walking is something that we have to observe, learn, remember, and then practice. Many species in the animal kingdom don't have this need. They fall onto the ground being able to walk. For humans, much of our ability is learned and practiced, including the ability to be silent.

Practice does not stop at just the ability to learn to be silent. Practice happens in other areas of our Stoic life as well. Asking questions, contemplating answers, and reflecting on actions are all acts that improve with practice. The difference between Stoics and non-Stoics is that Stoics practice with attention to what they are doing. That takes the benefits of practice further. A Stoic's practice is not blind repetition but rather conscious acts of perfection.

The more silence is practiced, allowing it to become the natural state of the Stoic instead of isolated events, it frees up valuable bandwidth in the brain. The increased bandwidth results in a better mind and improves the array of mind-sets.

It is not considered silence if only the lips refrain from activity. It requires that the mind also retreat from unnecessary chatter. When there is insufficient bandwidth because there is too much unnecessary input, the mind is unable to concentrate or have sufficient energy to engage in deep thought. A mind that engages in chatter will only be able to muster shallow thought, which will eventually determine the kind of activity it will then go on to seek.

Shallow thought begets further shallow thinking and subsequently only able to consume shallow content. Imagine if a person does not know how to engage in deep thought. How would they understand literature or plays that are deep and go beyond what is merely spoken and shown? A mind that can't understand deep content would prefer to refrain from that kind of content and will only stick to what is base and easily digestible. That propagates further shallow thinking. This kind of apathy is non-Stoic.

Once the mind is lethargic in the face of deep thought, it is unable to seek the truth in the nature of what is in front of its eyes. The world to the shallow thinker is binary in its choices— black or white, good or bad, right or wrong. Nuances are lost, long-term consequences are invisible, and one relies on the providence of luck to get beyond the fog of what they can't see. This is antithetical to Stoics.

A simple way to contrast the Stoic's world with the rest is that the Stoic seeks to understand the world around him beyond the shallow binary choices. A Stoic is all about the holistic understanding of the world because it is obvious to him that everything is connected. If this is true, then it is reasonable to the Stoic that everything is affected by something else. The compound influence, the domino effect, the chain reaction of all things is thought of as the nature of systems.

As he sees deeper and finds larger systems in his midst because he finds connections between a greater number of items in a larger orbit, he starts to recognize the face of an almighty power. He does not need to personify that power and make it look like a man, woman, beast, or plant, but he still understands that the fabric connecting everything even connects time, peace, features, and effects is all mighty, omnipresent, and all-pervasive.

In time, his view of God, spirituality, and the universe evolves, but the journey is not about one God, your God, my God, or the most powerful God. The Stoic transcends the personification of this all-pervasive presence and realizes that to better understand God all he needs to do is pursue the truth. Once he sees the truth in all things, that is where he finds God.

Stoics are the epitome of stability because they are not swayed by the vagaries of the distractions of the present moment or the worries of a future moment. They are the anchor that others need to withstand the tempest of the chaos of the world we live in. You can recognize a Stoic when you see one, and you can tell that he has the peace of the universe within him.

The single most accurate way to describe a Stoic is that he is one with his surroundings, and he is at peace with it. He may be wealthy or may live on the streets. Whichever he is, he is by choice and not the result of foolish means. His wealth is not gained by deception and neither is his poverty the result of loss by folly. A Stoic means to be where he is at any given point of his existence. He is a man of purpose.

A Stoic lives a different life from others not because he wants to be different but because he sees the world the way it is. In his effort to see the truth, he shuns the whitewash that is sometimes smeared over the realities of life. Instead, he chooses to see things in the way that lacks even the slightest prejudice, bias, or preconception. He sees things as they are.

Prejudice and preconception are required elements of the cognitive process. If we had no starting point, which by definition is a preconception, we would have no way to kick-start the cerebral process. The Stoic, when he was still a novice and the times prior, did engage in preconception, bias, and prejudice, but as he advanced, his set of notions improved, and so his preconception framework tended more to the truth than it did in the past. We can think of this as not having bias or preconception since they are not negative in nature but approximate the truth of the matter. These preconceptions, however, are merely the starting point. The Stoic is not lazy to stop there. He pushes forward so that he can then get to what is actually in front of him instead of what he first thought. The nature of the Stoic is not to believe that he is so right as to not be flexible in his determination.

Stoics do not shout from the mountaintop that they are Stoics and especially today in a world where Stoicism is being hawked and bartered as a form of solution to the problems of the world in return for glamour. It does have its solutions, but Stoicism itself is not the answer the world needs. It is not the miracle that answers all questions; in fact, it has no answers for us. As we have repeatedly stated, it is only a framework to understand the data stream and find the truth.

The world needs people who understand, and Stoicism gives people the tools to do that, but the crucial element of the whole solution is not the dogma or the commandments. It is the person. This is a collaborative effort to be done in solitary. Yes, it is paradoxical, but most truths in this universe are. It is collaborative because we need to have all senses and perspectives so that we can share the information each of us comes up with and then put that together by ourselves. For this to work, the more who understand, the better. Imagine a world where no one is swayed by greed and pleasure but rather motivated by contribution and contentment. What if everyone were interested in equity instead of riches, understanding instead of ignorance, perpetual happiness instead of momentary ecstasy?

Indeed, the world would be a better place.

To get under way in our quest to understand the Stoic, it is important that we leave behind all the values and sophistication of the material world and the world that promotes momentary highs over long-term happiness. It is necessary to lay open our values so that we are open to change if indeed change is necessary to be able to experience happiness.

It is also required for the novice who wants to understand Stoicism that he may end up being prosperous, wealthy, and revered, but under no circumstances can he covet those things when he starts his quest to understand Stoicism or at any point along his path. To do so would end his quest before it starts.

The Stoic has power over what he comes in contact with. It means that he has the power of understanding the limits to which he can manipulate the time and the extent to which the element will change him by coming into contact with him. The Stoic must understand what this power is, and it must be realized before the rest of the book even begins that power in no way is meant to subjugate others or other things. The power over things is the power over oneself and the way one perceives it, understands it, and understands the nature of all things.

The Stoic must also understand that all forces lie in balance and symmetry. One cannot raise oneself without expending effort to do so. One cannot extract something without giving up something else. One cannot become Stoic without giving up one's past. It is an infinite universe, but the laws of nature still govern it.

Two kinds of understanding relate to the topic at hand. The first is the ancient Stoic origins and evolution. Understanding the history of the philosophy helps with getting to know the essence of the philosophy and also prevents us from wasting time reinventing the wheel.

One should learn through philosophical texts and the historical record what has been passed down since the time of Socrates. While Socrates or the generation after him was not responsible for the philosophy of the Stoa Poikile, which was the early iteration of Stoicism, it was within the reasoning and teaching of Socrates that the eventual distillation of observations and hypothesis led to the new school of thought.

Chapter 1 - Chronology of the Beginning

"Man conquers the world by conquering himself."

Zeno of Citium, Founder of Stoicism

The Stoa Poikile, in direct translation, is the painted porch. It refers to the northern portion of the Agora in ancient Athens. The Agora was the common place where scholars and philosophers met to discuss ideas and philosophies. Socrates used to sit at the Agora discussing his ideas and listening to the thoughts and arguments of his students and followers.

In the ancient days of Athens, intellectual and academic advancement had taken hold of the city's learned class. They yearned for a better understanding of the world and the universe beyond. They were part academician, part historian, part philosopher, and part storytellers, all rolled into one using the logic of Socrates to investigate life and the most important questions it presented.

As they developed, Stoics began to value grammar and vocabulary in language. They brought this to Rome and helped develop the Latin that was spoken in the upper echelons of government and academics. They believed that language resulted in accurate recordkeeping of ideas and discussions as well as forming unambiguous communication among participants.

But the impetus and genesis of all critical thinking that went into developing Stoa germinated from the methods of Socrates and were carried by his students over the course of two hundred years.

Socrates

Socrates was a classical philosopher born in 470 BC, with a focus on the moral responsibility of man. Much of his ideas and reasoning eventually went on to become the basis for Western civilization and Western thinking.

One of the instruments that spread Western philosophy across Eastern lands was Alexander the Great, who was tutored both as a child and a young adult by Aristotle, a student of Plato. Plato learned directly under Socrates and went on to become one of his fiercest advocates, students, and biographer. As Alexander conquered the East, he took with him and planted the philosophy of the Greeks, which was rooted deeply by this point in the moral timber of Socrates' teaching.

Through his school of thought, which spurned all the other schools, Socrates was the prime mover in the framework of thinking. Many of the individual thought processes were in fact not from Socrates directly, but it was developed within the framework that he created.

Socrates advocated the power of contemplation and reflection. He was the philosopher who insisted that each person is responsible for the path he takes in his life, and that path needs to be subjected to the examination of one's own mind. Today, we call it contemplation and reflection. It is also the way we hold ourselves accountable for our actions. He did all this through the new form of analysis called dialectic reasoning. He would pose a series of questions on a subject until he arrived at a self-evident truth that could not be refuted. If he could do that, then he felt certain that his train of reasoning was the right one.

The Stoic principles that were the result of two hundred years of evolution from Socrates had been subjected to the power of the philosopher's mind from all walks of life. From men who were rich merchants to men who were slaves, they had all brought their perspectives to bear on the matter, which is one of the reasons why Stoicism has turned out to be a robust framework of living and coming in touch with the divine.

Socrates contributed a number of dimensions to the eventual Stoic framework. All of them are highly crucial to the development of the proper mind-set and the longevity of the resolve that sprouts from it. He believed that the answer and truth of all things lies within each of us, and we need contemplation and meditation to reveal those secrets.

Since the secrets are found within the soul, it makes sense that one has to maintain that soul and keep it in good order without any risk of being tarnished or corrupted. The soul is not some mystical ghost according to Socrates but rather some form of matrix of energy that encapsulates a dimension beyond that in which the body and all tangible elements occupy.

The equation is simple. The body supports the mind by giving it the energy that it needs and the mobility to touch all sorts of stimuli. The brain is the machine of observation that will gradually but surely reveal the existence of the soul, and the soul is connected to the energy of the universe. That path is as important as the existence of the soul. Without the journey from body to mind to spirit, we will never be able to come face-to-face with the face of the universe.

He also believed that we, not the call of man, are to evangelize his brethren. One is not here to evangelize or proselytize the teachings of reason, logic, or spirituality. Instead, one is here to act it out so that others can follow by example rather than do by force or coercion.

As such, the Socratic method became the blueprint of the subsequent schools of thought, from Plato's Academy School of Thought to Zeno's School of Thought that gave rise to Stoa Poikile.

The Socratic Method was used to decompose all ideas and experiences into a form that could be written or spoken for transmission and then spread among the masses. It became the Science of Dialogue and the foundation of logic.

It is this framework of logic and reason that sits at the heart of the Stoic. The Stoic is naturally measured in his language and deliberate in his tone to be able to communicate exactly what he means and not one shade more than is necessary. This is the same kind of Socratic style that has persisted for almost 2,400 years since the days of Socrates at the Agora.

That amount of time in existence does two things. The first is that it exposes and subjects the method to countless reviews and opinions over the course of time. If there is a flaw in the system, surely someone would have found it by this point, even if they were not trying to.

The second is that it stood the test of time. Over the last two and half millennia, the world and its societies have gone through major social and technological changes. If the strategy developed for thinking still works, then it must definitely have it right.

Beyond these first two issues, it is then apparent that the core of logic and reasoning had a significant amount of time to spread far and wide, and, more importantly, it had the opportunity to develop and mature.

It was thanks to Plato and all the other schools of thought that the Socratic method developed and that we are now able to see the world through Stoic eyes.

Plato

After Socrates' conviction and execution, it was Plato who took up the mantle and wrote numerous records of the contributions of Socrates. In those days, there were no historians—only philosophers and teachers. History was chronicled in narrative and story form, which, in time, slipped into myth and lore.

Some of the books that Plato wrote that are worth reading about Socrates include The Apology, Crito, Phaedo, and Euthyphro. They are worth reading if one is in the pursuit of happening the skills in thinking.

Plato was the man responsible for codifying, in his own way, the words of Socrates and perpetuated the framework that other thinkers then advanced. As such, it is core of Stoicism.

But that core didn't just go from Plato and Socrates to being the founding principles of Stoa. It went through at least two hundred years of refinement. That path is an interesting and critical part of the journey in embracing the Stoic framework and values.

But it was not just Plato that carried the Socratic baton to the next generation. There was Euclid of Megara who brought in his own ideas that were based on the mathematics of the day. Euclid was a mathematician who took logic and reasoning to a different level.

The school was known as the Megarian School of Thought, and it had some subtle differences compared with Plato's version of things. This was not a difference that was in opposition but one that enriched the framework. It served as the guardrails that protected the whole where the wilder ideas of Plato were brought into check.

They also brought an additional layer to the framework in terms of the idea to be good. Goodness was never an issue until this point. It was an arbitrary factor, and as you will see later in the book, good versus bad is not a good way to analyze things, but Euclid's version of good and wise was not an arbitrary measure of things. His version of good was the adherence to principles and morals as such the good that was discussed in his writings can be thought of as principled—something that is a lot more academic than the arbitrary understanding of good.

This is the start of the ethical and principled elements of Stoic virtues. The Megarian contribution to Stoic teachings came from sparks and debate that went on between Plato and Euclid. It was not a passive discussion around a table of cheese and wine. These were full-throated debates in the marketplace for all to hear. It was an intellectual clash of titans and formed the path that would eventually lead to the Stoic School of Thought.

After Euclid, his student Thrasymachus of Corinth took over and developed the Megarian School and then passed the reins to Stilpo, who was active about a hundred years after the death of Socrates.

The Cynics

Plato formed the first path from Socrates to Stoa, Euclid developed the second, parallel track, while the Cynics formed the third parallel track. It was formed by Antisthenes, another student of Socrates.

Antisthenes' school of thought brought the element of nature and the layer that nature is the during engine behind all tangible and intangible phenomena—static and dynamic.

The Cynics are not what is ordinarily thought of as what the word means in English today. It is not the references to cynical behavior or the practice of being cynical. The Cynics school of thought is more about the ability to observe nature and see how nature works and how it manifests. That same path and workings can be seen in all areas of life and all levels of it. They believe the life that is lived in harmony with nature is a life that is virtuous.

It is often mistaken that Cynics live in exclusion of comforts as a way to punish themselves and keep in line with their teaching, but this is not entirely accurate. Cynics separate themselves and comfort as a way to retain clarity and piety instead of being distracted by the complacency of comfort. It is something that has become part of the human condition. Our ancestors in the Paleolithic period would gorge themselves with food and then spend the next few days doing nothing. Once they were hungry again, they would become more active and industrious in order to go out and hunt again. It is a natural human tendency that the Cynics used as the prime motivation for their achievements.

It is also the first instance of minimalism that we see in Western history. It was the start of understanding how minimalism brings about clarity. This same idea still exists in deep Stoic literature and teachings. Happiness is found in the pursuit and contribution toward society in general, not from the hoarding of material wealth and objects that clutter the space around you and the mind within you.

The three schools that were briefly touched upon here, the Academic of Plato, Euclid's Megarian, and the Cynics, all combined their deeper understanding of the natural phenomenon of philosophy according to Socrates and formed the foundation of Stoa when Diogenes came along. Even though Diogenes himself was not the founder of Stoa, he did form the crucial link between the collaboration of the spin-offs from Socrates and all the individual advancements in thinking that were made after him.

Each step that came about was in tandem and then in sequence from the logical progression to understanding human interactions with the world around him, which was more than just the interaction with nature, but also the interactions with other humans and the interaction with knowledge itself. It became the fountain of curiosity and the framework to understand the fruits of that curiosity.

Take the contribution of the Cynics and their vein of minimalism that fed into the heart of the Stoa. What could minimalism possibly have to do with any of the teachings of Stoicism?

The answer lies in the fact that Stoicism considers distractions of desires and vanities to be a force that can derail a person's mind and prevent him from reaching what he is truly capable of and what he or she could otherwise achieve.

Happiness is not the result of the cessation of desire. Instead, it is the emptiness that the fulfillment of these desires result in. Look at the lives of those who win these multimillion-dollar lotteries. Not one of them (or close to it) has ever lived a happy life after getting the material windfall that they desired.

The other key concept of Antisthenes that made it into Stoicism is the notion that all of mankind is a brotherhood. We are all connected beyond borders and languages. This brotherhood of man was more important to him than any man-made divide. Man was not differentiable because of the tone of his skin, the swagger of his tongue, or the content of his rituals. We were all one and the same. This contribution to Stoa resulted in Stoics realizing and understanding that racism and bias are not acceptable and only reside in the mind of the weak. It was the same line of reference that Martin Luther King Jr embodied when he uttered, "They will not be judged by the color of their skin but by the content of their character." This line of thought was then taken on by the infamous Diogenes, who even had Alexander the Great's total respect and admiration.

Diogenes

Diogenes was known as the mad version of Socrates. If he came in front of you today, you would find every excuse to exit the area. Diogenes embraced minimalism to a degree that was extreme. While the intention of the Stoic was not to go that far, Diogenes does us great service by showing us the virtues of minimalism in thought and living.

He understood that simplicity was a new level of enlightenment and expounded the notion that possessions are distractions. If truth was found in focus, then nothing that detracted one from focus should be entertained.

He also believed that it was not just possessions that created distractions. He also believed that a vast array of human vanity, from power to wealth to prestige and fashion, were all distractions from leading a virtuous and enlightened life. As such, he rejected all those things and chose an almost ascetic life. While there is no deep benefit that we can gain for that in today's life, his doing so gives us deep insight into its effects. We can learn from it and institute parts of it in our daily life, which is what the foundations of Stoa did as things progressed.

Before long, his progression in thought and action landed him naked on the streets of Athens, begging for food during the day, mocking the richer men who walked by, and living in a barrel at the entrance of the marketplace. When nature called, the brash Diogenes would just go wherever he felt like it without a second thought. Revolting? Yes, but it portrays a man who had shed all notion of what others may or may not think of him. It was not any of these shenanigans that endeared him to the people but instead was his loyalty to the truth and the revulsion of all else.

From Diogenes, the teachings of the Cynic passed to Crates of Thebes. Crates, a wealthy man, embraced the teachings of the Cynic School and gave away all his possessions in exchange for a life on the streets of Athens. He was joined by his wife, who subscribed to his philosophy. Crates was respected in Athens just as his teacher was and was constantly given food by those who passed him on the street.

With time he had a following of students who also gave up their possessions, and the group would sit by the street discussing the philosophy of the ages and the politics of the day. One such student to join this group was a young man by the name of Zeno, who came from nearby Citium (pronounced as see-Shum).

Zeno

Zeno was born around 336 BC and lived near the town of Larnaca in southwestern Cyprus. It was a place of Semitic influence amidst the Greek culture. In his time, it was called Kition, the Greek word for Citium, which was Latin.

Zeno was a rich merchant by the time he heard of Crates of Thebes. He worked for his father, who himself was a rich merchant plying the Mediterranean Sea and trading from ports as far as way as Spain to ones in exotic Africa. His father frequently stopped in Athens for the express purpose of locating gifts for his family. For his son, he would bring pamphlets and books to quench his almost insatiable thirst for knowledge.

Among Zeno's reading list were such books as Plato's Republic, Xenophon's Memorabilia, and other texts by prominent writers of the time.

As he matured, Zeno developed his own ideas. It was an amalgamation of many of the different schools of thought since he had read almost all of them and found a way to combine them and see a deeper sense of truth in the combined teachings of all the schools that spawned from Socrates two hundred years before.

Just as his father had stopped in Athens on his trade voyages across the Mediterranean, Zeno, too, started to stop in Athens when he was old enough to sail as part of the trade he did for the family. Instead of merely stopping to buy gifts, he started attending sessions that were conducted along the streets and in the Agora.

On one of those times he was in Athens in a bookshop, he inquired where he could learn more and whose teachings he should listen to while he was in Athens. Fate would have it that Crates was right across the street from the bookstore, and the Athenian bookseller pointed him across the street to Crates.

Zeno was thirty years old at this time. After listening to Crates on a number of different occasions, he was so convinced and elated at the same time that he joined him.

With that the sparks that would give rise to the flame of Stoa were born. In a about a dozen years after that, Zeno began teaching his iteration of the teachings that had evolved since the time of Socrates. He went on to take up residence in the north part of the Agora where the painted porch was located, and people in the Agora started referring to the school that met there as the Painted Porch. In Greek, that was Stoa Poikile, which gradually became the Stoa and then went on to become Stoicism.

Chapter 2 - Power to Perceive and Discern

"If you are distressed by anything external, the pain is not due to the thing itself, but to your estimate of it; and this you have the power to revoke at any moment."

Marcus A Aurelius, Roman Emperor

The best place to find the answers one seeks is to look for them in plain sight. Everything we need is all around us, and we just have to open our proverbial eyes to see. We cannot rely on just the senses that we have because each sense on its own is only a fraction of the total information that is captured, and even then it is not enough. A bomb that detonates a hundred feet away can be seen, heard, felt, smelled, and (if close enough) tasted—that is all five senses to give you a complete picture. But is it a complete picture? At that point, you only have the profile of the event. You only know the "what" and the "where." How about the "how" and the "why"? Instead of standing a hundred feet away, what if one were to stand farther back—perhaps one thousand feet away from ground zero. Then there is less information that can be captured by each sense. One may still be able to visually observe it and possibly hear it, but feeling it and smelling it may not happen, and tasting it in the air probably won't happen either. As you keep moving farther away, placing greater distance between you and the event, the less any single sense seems to be effective.

The increasing distance between the observer and the event represents a movement in space. A second alteration in the spatial dimension happens when you remain at the same distance and alter your relative position to the event. Where you stand relative to the event gives you perspective. How far you stand from the event increases or decreases the amount and quality of the sensory data that you receive.

What if you move away in time? Moving away in time means that you are further away from the event in time, which is to say that if you come before or after the event, you will not be able to observe it with the same set of senses any longer.

If you arrive a little before, the event hasn't happened. If you come a little later, the event would have already occurred.

The timing makes a significant difference in your ability to discern the event. If you come after the event, you may be able to see the effects of the event, but if you come before the event, even the aftereffects are not there for you to forensically observe and make a determination of the event. So not only does it matter if you are in physical unison with the event but that you are also in temporal unison for your senses to capture the information.

All this makes your senses alone unreliable in seeking out the information that you need to understand the truth of all things. What makes the difference is using your mind to discern the how, where, why, and when. It's not enough that your eyes capture the event. Your mind has to make sense of it. You can either stop at seeing something with your eyes, or you can proceed deeper and discern the same event with your mind. The latter is the richer experience and the one that Stoics engage in in all they take part in.

The power of the Stoic comes from the sharpened mind that he has and the framework that he uses in observing past, present, and future events. It is the mind, not the brain, not the eyes, nor the ears, or any one of the remaining three senses that gives the Stoic his ability to observe, discern, and understand before going on to act in a way that creates the optimal outcome.

The fundamental purpose of the Stoic is to find and understand the truth so that he may act in accordance with it. That fundamental purpose gives rise to the mind and body that the Stoic needs to be able to achieve his purpose.

The chapter started out claiming that all we need to understand and perceive the world is around us. The only thing we need to do is bring our trained mind to it and allow it to observe and cogitate. Once we realize that it is the mind that can see the truth, it will become your most cherished asset and most powerful ally.

Direct Power

We have power, for instance, over what happens in our future, but we have no power over what has happened in our past. We have power over what happens in our presence (not present), but we have no power over what happens beyond our reach. That alone creates a long list of combinations that vary in gradations and effectiveness. Some not so far, some further, some in the recent past, and some much earlier.

The Stoic knows that he has direct power over what happens right here and now. Whatever happens in the future or beyond our immediate reach is indirect power, and it is treated differently. By knowing there is a difference in what one can control and what one can't, the Stoic starts to formulate a set of values. He knows that once a wave of consequences begins to form and it gains critical mass, there is no way of controlling it, and so he avoids things that will have negative consequences in the future by making sure he sticks to good practices in the present. This is direct power over the present and indirect power over the future.

Once he can control everything he can control, then what remains is what he cannot absolutely control. These are things that he leaves alone. By "leaving it alone," it is meant to stress that he does not even worry about it. Worry is a distraction that serves no purpose. If you can mitigate the effects of what you cannot control, then by all means proceed on that path. Do the best you can and then avert your attention to what you can control and extract the good from that.

What we have to take from this is that there are two distinct issues that we can categorize. The Stoic sees these as things that one can control and those things one can't. There is a third layer that happens to be the boundary layer between the things one can control and the things one can't. In other words, there are things that could one day come under his control if he works toward it.

In most cases, most well-adjusted people can appreciate the difference between the things they can control and the things they can't, but yet they still make many mistakes. Stoics are better at this because they observe and then stick to it. They have the discipline to put into motion the actions they plan. The rest either can't distinguish between what they can control or do not have the discipline to stay grounded in the present and control what they can.

There is a third aspect to what can be controlled and what can't. There are groups of things that may not be in one's control today but can be if one applies the necessary effort or enough time passes by. This is the boundary layer where things can go either way.

That boundary layer is where we usually make the mistakes that determine the suffering in our life. In some cases, it is also the things that we make the mistake of thinking that we have control over but actually don't and the things that we think that we have no control over but actually do.

Knowing what we control and what we don't is an important part along the path of the Stoic. If we remember that our mind is our most valuable asset, then we should be careful where we deploy it. If we deploy it toward tasks that it has no control over, we are wearing it down for no benefit. If we apply it to things we can control, then the effect is powerful, and the mind increases in ability.

This is not to say that we should not attempt things that we do not yet know how to handle. That is not the same thing. It is also the reason why study and expanding the mind and its abilities are an important part of the Stoic's path.

This boundary layer that we mentioned earlier is the layer that exists to separate the areas that we can control and the areas that we can't. The two sides (the universe of things we can control and the universe of things we cannot control) in any given moment of time are fixed, but the events in the boundary layer are not fixed. They can alter back and forth depending on circumstances.

Take, for instance, one's choice of food. As a baby, we have no control over the food we eat. That event is squarely in the realm of the uncontrollable part of our life and can't be changed in that moment in time. As we grow older and our skill levels change, we are able to alter the food we ingest—from formula to solid food to different cuisines to different categories, and so on. The boundary layer over the things we can control in food changes in time and moves between what we can control and what we can't.

This simple illustration and example can be applied to a number of different areas as well. However, there are some things that lie squarely in both ends—things we can control and things we can't. On the one end are such events as birth and death that we can't control. On the other hand, there are events that we can control, one of which is consequences. This is the indirect control that we talked about. The issue is that they are controlled indirectly in the future by controlling directly what is in the present.

One of the effects of understanding nature and familiarizing the mind with the consequence of actions is that the Stoic is able to present or promote his actions based on the consequences he wants to avoid or the outcomes he wants to experience. It is important to make the point that considerable effort should be expended to know exactly what is in one's control, what is not, and what can be brought under control with concerted effort applied.

For the most part, we can control most consequences that arise from our own actions and reactions. As long as we play a part in the sequence of events, we will have a hand in determining how the consequences unfold. A small percentage of it may lie along the boundary layer, but for a large part of it they exist squarely in the section of things that we can control. The one thing a Stoic knows is that the consequences that take place tomorrow are typically based on the actions taken today (or the lack of actions).

The Stoic also knows that once you get all the elements that you can control in your control most of the things in life work out well. What remains that is outside your control will not hurt you if you realize that things that happen outside your control are not things that you should feel bad about.

In this respect, the Stoic realizes that he should do whatever he can today so that the consequences of his actions lead him to a life that is better off tomorrow than it is today. A Stoic is highly proactive and takes control of his life in all areas that he can control but nothing more.

A Stoic does not seek to control things that are not in his control because he knows that the attempt of trying to control things that are not in his control results in consequences in itself. The first is that because he has finite time controlling or attempting to control things that he inevitably has no control overtakes his resources away from the things that he can control. That compounds the negative consequences.

The second is that he learns not to expect things that he cannot control. If he can't control the weather tomorrow, he is not going to expect sunshine for his enjoyment or rain for his crops. He is going to take it as it comes and leave the resources of his mental faculties intact because he would not have to spend time worrying about it.

There is a second area of concern among Stoics. It is about mitigating the effects of things that are outside the sphere of control. To put it simply, you can't control the weather, but you can mitigate its effects to a certain extent. Take, for instance, the current change in climate. Being a part of the solution is an interesting way to think, but it is not going to ameliorate your immediate predicament caused by it. As such, you need to take steps to counter the effects, and if you are a person who thinks in the long term, then maybe you should take steps to not contribute to the degradation but takes steps to get through it. Whatever you can do to mitigate climate change is not the issue. That is a different topic for a different book, but the point here is that you should be able to take steps if you know that a certain consequence is making its way to you whether or not you were the cause of it. A Stoic always has his eyes and ears open and his mind engaged.

If you have a farm and the climate is degrading, then maybe you could dig a well to supply your crops with water. Waiting for something and giving up saying that it is not in your control is not the way of the Stoic. A Stoic does indeed know what is in his control and what is not, but that does not mean that they do not try to find a way to mitigate those issues.

To be able to do this, a Stoic usually spends time in study and contemplation. These are the two tools of the Stoic. The more the Stoic studies and the more he thinks, the more he is able to push the boundary layer further into the territory that was once out of his control. The Stoic knows that many things that he is unable to control alter as he spends time in study and in contemplation. That is just one of the reasons why you find the Stoic usually silent. His mind is always animated, and to do this his mouth must not be.

A Stoic knows that talking takes a lot of energy and resources. It removes time from thinking, and it removes resources from contemplating, and thus the person who talks gradually becomes an empty vessel because the factor of time that has been applied to the effort of talking has taken away from thinking, and the less one thinks, the less his spoken word is of value. As such, the more one talks, the more unworthy he becomes. Silence is a major part of the Stoic's being.

Total silence—the kind that is not spent in the pursuit of advancement—is not productive. Total silence shifts the balance of the mind as it becomes less interested to seek out the truth. There should be a good balance between thought and speech. A Stoic typically spends 0.5 percent of his time in talk, if needed, and 99.5 percent of his time in thought and action. Many Stoics, in fact, dedicate a full day every week to silence, meditation, contemplation, and reflection.

This is the reason why Stoics are highly effective people. Think about such men as Marcus Aurelius and Seneca. They lived extremely rich and fruitful lives, and their actions and words spilled over into our own time. They tell us if we take the time to read their secrets and understand their words in the way they intended.

Once you look at life as the battle between everything you can control and everything you can't, then you apply the same notion that you control all that you can and do not waste time with things that you can't, and you are forced to take responsibility for your life. It is highly unfair to the Almighty to blame him for the malady in one's life because all the control that one has been squandered in worry over things that one had no control over.

Take the issue of death. A Stoic looks at death in a very simple way. He has made a contract with providence the day he enters this world that says that he will one day die in the future. He didn't have control over the entry and in most cases does not have control over the exit. He himself is not sad about it, but the persons who meet him and rely upon him are sad that he dies even though no promise whatsoever had been made that he would live forever.

No one has rightful control over the end of life. It comes when it comes. To be sad about it and to worry about it is neither fruitful nor Stoic. A Stoic makes preparations for his end of life long before and then just goes about the time he has by making the most of it. His resolve is to fulfill his time on earth to make it and to experience it in the best way he can.

A Stoic's sense of morality is very different from any other's. He does not think to himself that he is bound by moral or ethical actions but by actions that will have a consequence on his tomorrows. He is very certain that the reason he does not get drunk today is because he knows he will face the consequences of a hangover tomorrow. He does not refrain from drink today because he is told to by some inexplicable law or the pious morality of someone else.

Members of the Greek elite who attended Plato's parties would say that not only did they have a good time but also that they had a good time the next day because they did not have to nurse a hangover. There is no rule among Stoics that says that one should not drink, but most Stoics do not gravitate toward inebriated living because it dulls the mind and wastes time. It's not about morality or ethics. It's about functionality and consequence.

This the power of the Stoic. It takes time to develop this habit. To see the act from the perspective of the consequence. We can sometimes think of this as the life driven by purpose. For what is purpose if not a set of stated goals that need to be achieved? And what are goals if not the foresight of consequences to the underlying action? If you want to be a doctor, then you need to study medical books. If you want to study medical books, then you have to understand chemistry and biology. If you want to study chemistry and biology, you have to know science, and so on. You can trace this back to learning your ABCs when you were a child, and that action in the moment resulted in a consequence that formed the basis of the next action and the next after that until you reached the goal you set. But the action that you took, the matter that you can't the power over was in the present moment at each stage of your life.

Once you understand your set of consequences, you can trace your path from your current position to the end, and that becomes the core value of your existence. The Stoic's life is focused on the present moment so that he can sail through life and be of use to the world he lives in.

Epictetus, the slave philosopher, is the master of this distinction between what is in our control and what is not. He clearly understands the differences that separate the two, and as you read his writings, it starts to become obvious that he is onto something.

For instance, when we are certain that something is not in our power, there are two things that we can do with it. The first is that we can put it aside and find a path that mitigates the factors or magnifies it. If it is a negative issue that brings about harm, yet we have no control over it, then we find action that could mitigate the consequence. In this case, we seize control over the outcome of an uncontrollable situation. On the other hand, if there is a bounty that is coming to us and we can't increase it at the source, maybe we can do something that magnifies its effect by the time it gets to us. Both strategies are based on things that we can do to put us in a better position.

A Stoic's path is always being altered and optimized by his constant and vigilant evaluation of events and abilities. Over time the continuous evolution of our abilities and the experience that we gain from trial and error give the Stoic his expanded power set, and he finds that he has moved the line of skirmish closer to the end zone.

If someone like Marcus Aurelius were alive today, it is not hard to see how football (American football) would be one of his favorite sports. He would be able to see the philosophical angle of the game where two forces keep the game in balance and inch toward to the final game constantly trying, failing, getting up and heading for the end zone. That is a Stoic's way to life. He has no time for anything else.

As each step is fought for and won, in the midst of absolute focus and visualization of the outcome, the line of skirmish moves toward the end zone in favor of the player who is most into the game, the most prepared, and the most focused. The winner is the most deserving of the title. There is no bias—just the laws of nature and the laws of the human spirit in full display until the winner emerges. The Stoic sees this in all things.

For a Stoic, life is about a series of battles and skirmishes in which he puts his set of skills and experiences gained from the point of birth across all the times of failures and study and put against the forces of the present event. When the game is done, he then goes over the entire series of events that made up the game and reflects on it . . . one play at a time and he understands how he reacts, how he thought, how he interacted, and how he felt. Each event is an opportunity for the Stoic to sharpen his skills for the next game, where his abilities could be the sum of all experiences up to that point in the future.

Marcus Aurelius was one of the wisest generals in the battles that he undertook with his co-emperors (yes, there were two emperors during his time; they shared powers). His ability to strategize in battle was not widely known only because he was better known as the philosopher instead of being known as the general. It was a title that he was certain to prefer as well.

Once there was nothing to battle, he reigned over a time of peace that had not yet been seen by Rome. He did not shun war under the guise of philosophy. He was very clear within the four corners of his own mind that war was a necessary evil that had its purpose. War has its powers, and life in the wake of war has its benefits. For this reason, he determined that it was better to go to war to advance the political imperatives of the empire than it was to sit back and let barbarianism spread.

In this context, the philosophy of Stoicism and the tenets of religions, which Stoicism is often compared to, does not add up. If Stoicism is ideal, why does one accept the possibility of war? That is the usual question. Isn't war immoral? Isn't war unethical since it involves death, deception, and suffering?

The question that is posed is false. The Stoic sees past the surface of war where there might be carnage and suffering and looks at the net effect of a war that seeks to install peace in its wake. Would anyone disagree that Allied Forces that landed on the beaches of Normandy did more good than harm? Is war not a good thing when it is done to pursue higher values? That is the way Stoics see everything. They would not go to war to expand power for the sake of riches, but they would go to war to expand the sake of the common good over the long term.

The power over things that the Stoic sees is in the way that he has power over something or a group of events and the areas where he has no power over it. He then sees the line that demarcates it, and he sees that line as an organic and evolving line than encompasses the events that are something in one's control and not at other times. A Stoic is constantly on a quest to gain the skills necessary to push that line forward until the very end. He then comes to the point that there are only a few events that remain outside his control.

Death

Death remains outside the control of the Stoic, but the Stoic moves ever so closely to even solving that one final issue. Many eventually figure it out. Stoics realize that death is not the end. When they come to this, they realize it is not death that is the event they can't control, but the perspective of death is what they can control.

The need to control death only arises when one does not know what death is. Knowledge of death and the knowledge of life are two sides of the same coin. The moment the Stoic understands death it helps him to understand living. That raises the quality of his life.

In most cases, novices see death as something that cannot be controlled, and we find that death is the ultimate end point. The true Stoic comes to the realization, hopefully some time before the seemingly final event, that death is not the end, but merely the beginning. As such, the Stoic starts to see that he does not need to control it but rather needs to surrender to it. He comes to the realization that death is merely a change of state, and that whatever the state is beyond the effect of death it no longer concerns the state of the living.

The Stoic sees death as a necessary condition of life. Without the possibility of death, there is no possibility of life. Imagine if you could live for a million years without ever changing. Would that make your life any better? What is it about death that dominates the psyche of most people? The

Stoic believes that the fear of death comes from the fear of the unknown. The fear of the unknown comes from the fact that death indicates the annihilation of the senses. Death is the ultimate terminus for all the sensations one receives from the world around him as he knows it. No more sight, sound . . . this can instigate fear.

Most people think of death in a way that is final, and they think they would be able to do so much more if only they were able to live forever. The Stoic sees things differently. They realize that how much contribution they make to the world around them is not a function of the time they spend on this earth. The greatest conqueror on earth around 300 BC lived a few days before his 33rd birthday. By that time, Alexander the Great had conquered all of Persia and up to the northern part of India. He was the wealthiest man on the planet, and he brought civilization and culture to the barbarian worlds of the East. He did so much more in twelve years (he started his quest at the age of twenty-one) than most people do in the eighty years they live. It's not about how much time you spend in life. It's about how much living you do in that time.

This is the extent that the Stoic has figured out. In other words, he has conquered death. He conquers death because he realizes after much contemplation that death is not the final point and the terminus. It is merely an event like any other event. In some cases, you can control the event, and in some cases you cannot. Altering the event or mitigating the uncontrollable event is not how you placate the conversation of death. Instead, the Stoic looks at death and understands that the goal of life is to find all the tools that he accumulates along the way so that he can then overcome his own mind's notion of death.

Loss

Loss is a related issue in the discussion of death and the Stoic's power over things. There is the other side of the subject. Death is not always about one's own death. It could be the death and loss of a loved one. Sometimes, that hurts even more. A true Stoic works up to that. The loss of one's loved one and the pain that follows is a human frailty that the Stoic seeks to overcome, and most of them do because they see the truth of the matter and understand the core aspect of living.

To overcome loss, the Stoic realizes that there are three elements to it that need to be understood. The first is expectation followed by delusion and finally by attachment. A Stoic learns to minimize and abolish all three.

The loss of a loved one is usually painful because they fill our hearts and minds with their presence. We are able to fill our mind and time with the words and their presence so much so that we miss them when the expectation of those words and presence is absent. What if we didn't see that person as someone who satisfied a craving or filled our minds in selfish ways? What if we saw them as just a person? What if we didn't rely on their presence for our personal needs but rather contributed to them when they were in our midst? What if we didn't expect anything of them in the future and were grateful for them for the things that they brought into our life in the past? The answer is that we have zero expectations when they pass.

Missing someone is more about the cessation of expectations and the sudden termination of the thing that we are used to. If we can start to learn how to deal with the loss of a loved one, it brings us closer to the Stoic way of life than anything thing else in the experience of one's life. The ability to face loss and emerge is an event that grows us rather than diminishes us.

The largest part of a Stoic's life is to look at things in the present and carry the experience of the present moment into the future—nothing else. The expectation of receiving the same event in the future is both greedy and unrealistic. Heraclitus said that man does not step into the same river twice because the man has changed, and the river is no longer the same. This is one of the basic tenets of the Stoic. He understands that each moment is a new event to be experienced based on the contemplation of the past, but he is not meant to expect the past to repeat just because he feels safe that that is what he knows. Be open to the future, learn from the past, but remain and work in the present.

But the reason we feel loss is because we expect things to always be the same. We expect that the river that we dip our toes into will always be like the last time we experienced the waters of the river.

When we do that, we're missing out on living life. First of all, we are not looking beyond to the next event and constantly looking to experience a rerun of the past event. The second is that we are not opening ourselves to a new experience to be able to expand our mind and therefore our living.

Why do we miss that our children are growing up instead of looking forward to our grandchildren? Because we are constantly trying to step back into the same river that we know was good before. It is a lazy way of living life, and it is not the way the Stoic chooses to experience the world and the events that happen around him.

There is much to be learned about being a Stoic by looking at the hypothetical situation of losing the person that one currently loves. This loss does not need to be that which is caused by death alone. It can even be the loss of a child who goes off to college or gets married. What about the natural progression of things? Did we think they were not going to happen? Will a lawn that has been mowed stay trim? No. A time will come when it would need to be tended to again. This is how the Stoic sees all things. He is not delusional of what will happen and does not rely on luck to make things out of control come to fruition. If it does work in his favor, he will be grateful, but he will not expect that it happens again. This is why Stoics are accused of being cold. They are not cold. They are pragmatic and know clearly what they are getting into before they get into it. Nothing surprises them because they know what will happen, and there is no need to be surprised.

In the next chapter, we will look at the parallel between what we have typically called karma in the mainstream and how that meshes with

Stoicism in practice. There is a significant reason why Stoics and karma can be at odds with each other and why the karma that we think about in Stoic terms is more about the consequences of things rather than the retribution of past actions.

Stoics understand that it is not an individual perspective that makes up the world. It is the collective perspective, thought, and actions that give life to some of the nastiest things that have become part of the historical record in civilization.

Think about Nazi Germany between WWI and WWII. It is very easy to start off by saying that it was pure evil and that nothing can explain it. While there is no room to condone what happened, the central premise is that the atrocities came from the hatred of one man who represented a minority of the German public. What has that to do with Stoicism? Well, his idea was to bring purity and to rid the populace of anyone who didn't look like him or what he thought would be the ideal person. Hitler was devout in his religion. He was not a stupid man, but despite his intelligence and religious beliefs, he pushed too far with his zeal for purity. The excess of purity is in itself a bad direction to take because too much purity is, by definition, the lack of balance.

Balance

Between purity and balance, the Stoic always chooses balance, which is the most important measure of all things. Without balance, the harmony in which the universe exists is disrupted. The same within the universe in which the Stoic lives. Imagine trying to kill every last bacteria that exists on your skin. That imbalance promotes the growth of unfavorable bacteria and more problems down the road. Imagine studying all day without any time for play. Remember that all work and no play makes Jack a dull boy, as the old adage goes. Imagine eating only meat and not having any vegetables. These unbalanced situations project situations that make the mind realize that balance is always better than absolutely one way or the other.

What the Stoic understands about balance is that it is a lagging phenomenon. We are never really in a state of total balance. We are more in the constant pursuit of that balance. It is like the swinging pendulum. That pendulum is constantly searching for the balance between momentum of the swing and the force of gravity acting on the weight. Each time the balance is approached the momentum carries it further and the balance has to be hunted for again.

The universe is also a product of the hunting for balance. The momentary imbalance at the time of the Big Bang is what caused the explosion of space, matter, and time. Without that momentary imbalance, there would not be the expansion of the universe, which is still happening today in search of balance. If that balance is reached, everything stops.

The pendulum is the perfect analogy for the balance in life—being always in search of that balance allows us to progress and move forward. It is the pursuit of that balance that gives life and maintains life. Balance is the ultimate arbiter of all events and all situations. Even weather events happen because nature is trying to seek balance.

The animation in our lives is the same cascade toward balance. We keep seeking the balance of emotions, the balance of state, and the balance that represents peace in our lives. Within that cascade, we are driving by numerous factors, some of which we may not like and others that we love.

Perspective

We see the world sometime arc in that direction. Stoics do not see it that way. Look at Epictetus. He was a slave. Yet, much of his work influenced the thinking of Emperor Marcus Aurelius. Imagine that the fruit of a slave's mind influenced the thoughts and actions of a Roman emperor. How would that have worked out if Marcus Aurelius did not bother to read the writings of a slave? Would Hitler have done that?

The mind of a Stoic is vastly different from the mind of other philosophers. It is one of the reasons why it has resulted in such reverence in the minds of other observers. There is no enforcement of ideals and morals in Stoicism. There are only clear observations and understanding of consequences; after all, that is the reason the mind exists.

Run a thought experiment if you can. Think about the effect that it would have on your life if you only had a memory span of one waking moment. That means when you go to bed at night and wake up in the morning all your memories from the day before are erased. You start back up with no bias, no sense of self, and no care for anything of perceived value. You just wake up and find something to fill your belly. Meet the neighbors for the first time and go about your business. As soon as you fall asleep, all that you laughed about, all that you cried about, and all that you worry about get erased. Tomorrow, you start back up with a new slate.

What would happen in this kind of world? For one thing, you would have no worries. You would forgive those who have harmed you, and you certainly wouldn't begrudge someone for something that wouldn't matter. Would you have any care at that point?

Probably not.

Now imagine if you had a super memory. You remember every last detail. You remember everything someone said to hurt or offend you. How would you feel the moment you wake up the next day and see that person's face again? All those thoughts of pain would come rushing back. On the other hand, if you have long-term memory resiliency, you could make such technological advancements from one day to the next, building on your past achievements rather than having to reinvent the wheel each day.

These are two extremes that happen. No one is squarely in either corner, but we mostly tend to occupy one of the other areas with a degree of regularity. We each have patterns that we repeat over time, and the repetition itself perpetuates the mistakes and the consequences that we try to avoid. A Stoic does not do this. A Stoic sees the gift of memory as a tool to remember selective issues. He would rather remember those things that would advance him and bring him better consequences tomorrow than remember the issues that would bring him pain and eventual suffering.

Stoics believe in the power of choice, and thus they embrace the power over things that they have. You don't have to be ordained as a Stoic or live your life on the streets of Greece as the philosophers of old to be able to understand this. The power to be a Stoic lies in the selection of things you remember. You can choose to remember all the good, choose to brood over all the bad, or choose to forget everything and start fresh.

Stoics pick. They selectively take what will give them better consequences for tomorrow and discard the rest. That is the power of perspective. You don't have to see all things through rose-colored glasses. You only need to see things in a way that will give you the net benefit in the end. That is the purpose of perspective.

The question then arises about the perspective we control versus the truth that we don't. Are the two aspects of a Stoic's life inconsistent?

This section only exists because the novice often feels that perspectives and truth are inconsistent with each other. They are not, but the question is a fair one. The world tends to see the truth as opposite from perspective. If one sees the truth and it is consistent with what his neighbor sees, then the two of them have come close or have stumbled onto the truth, but the equation of any truth can be subjective in the eyes of the beholder.

Think about the story of the seven blind men and the elephant. The story is a hilarious one that depicts the state of the human condition. Seven blind men were introduced to an elephant one day. None of them had ever come across an elephant before. They did not know what to expect. The seven men were led to various stations around the large beast, and the blind men proceeded to inspect their target. When they were done, they were sat down and asked to describe the elephant. The first man, who had been standing by the large ears of the elephant, said that the elephant was like a big bat. To his amazement, everybody disagreed, and the next man to speak, who had been at the tail, said that it was more like a small snake. To this, the man who inspected the trunk said that it was indeed like a snake but not a little one. It was large and long.

This went on for some time with each man describing it in his own way—never agreeing or finding common ground in the impression of each other. Finally, they all left the company of their friends in disgust and went about their merry way never really getting to know what the truth was. Each man was satisfied with his own impression.

In the same way, all the perspectives we hear about and our perspectives of ourselves are never the same and have different shades of the same topic. Some shades are absolutely inconsistent, or so it may seem, and some disparities are close but not identical. If we choose to see it in absolute terms and forget that each person on earth brings with them the rich value of their perspective, we are then open to greater understanding of the universe—the overarching truth.

Where we stand, how we see things, and how we interpret the truth are not just a function of truth itself but a function of our own experiences and perspectives. We have to understand this aspect of the truth and its appearance in light of our perspective.

This chapter on the power over things that the Stoic comes into contact with is one that touches on a number of areas that are not easily grappled with and require reflection and understanding. It will not be easy to incorporate the matters discussed here into one's own life without repeated reading and exposure and then constant reflection and contemplation. The notion of direct power and the perspectives of death and loss as well as the need for balance and the comparison of the truth to perspective is designed to give the novice the necessary tools to chew on as he determines the next steps to take in his quest.

Chapter 3 - Karma and Stoicism

Karma has been used in many of the religions and philosophies that have dominated Eastern schools of thought. It has come to take on mainstream exposure in the last half century, and that has allowed the world to spill over from Sanskrit-based cultures into the Latin-based cultures in a way that has concomitantly brought about new realizations while spreading some misconceptions.

There is a deeper understanding of the concept in Sanskrit and in Greek and how it comes about in a person's life. Pop culture looks at karma as more of a comeuppance—a cosmic tit for tat. Karma says that if you have committed bad deeds and harbor bad intentions, then the universe will set you on a path of retribution. It is not so sinister as that, or simple, for that matter.

There is no equivalent of karma in Stoicism if you look at things on the surface. One is not punished for immoral acts, and one is not doomed by the mistakes he or she makes. Stoicism looks at this subject in a pragmatic way just as the Buddhists and the ancient Vedics do, but they look at it in a way that is deeper and insightful.

The equivalent of karma in Greek is a term that many would have come across. It is the word "logos." You may have seen it as part of the triumvirate of perfect persuasion skills—logos, ethos, and pathos. The word "logos" in linguistics is carried into philosophy with a slightly different meaning.

Logos, or put simply in the context of philosophy, is about the process of reasoning within the mind. It is the art of self-contemplation that leads to answers, more questions, then deeper answers, until finally arriving at the insight that is needed to see the universe and the world around you beyond binary choices.

The art of self-contemplation is found in no other creation of nature than within the human mind. Can a tree know itself? Could water understand its role in life? Could critters in the forest contemplate their actions? None of these occurrences in nature is able to look inward and understand its own existence. In fact, neither can your hand or your eyes. Your eyes will not be able to look at themselves in the mirror and understand what it is.

You have the ability to contemplate because of two separate areas in your psyche. The first is your ability to observe patterns, and the second is your ability to imagine forward. This ability is both beneficial and problematic. It is beneficial because we can game out our actions and get a good idea of what the consequences of an action would be. It is problematic because it can cause unnecessary stress when we game out all the improbable situations and cause the mind to take on a state of fear and worry.

Everything is Connected

It is easy to see in physical terms how everything is connected, but the connection goes far beyond the physical continuity that exists. It isn't just that this universe is made up of the same material everywhere you go—just in different combinations and quantities. But the energy that exists in all objects and inside all forces is the fabric that lies as the substrate of all existence.

The closest way to imagine this is the intricate weave of fabric that makes up various patterns of the fabric. It's a good way to see it, but the universe is also connected by a fabric that is undetectable by any of the usual senses that allow us to see, hear, and smell.

More than any physical attribute that we can think of to be connected, we have to realize that our actions, the intangibles in this universe, are also connected. We often think of tangibility as something that cannot be detected by the senses. For most of this book, we will leave that definition intact except for this section, where we will momentarily depart from it. The connection that we refer to as intangible is also the connection that we cannot describe without much contemplation on the part of the novice.

Imagine the feeling you get when someone is looking at you when your back is turned. There is no sensor in you that can pick up on that, yet many people can get the feeling that someone is watching them. When you think of someone far away and then some time that day or the next that person calls or shows up—have you ever experienced that? That is one of the elements of the connection. A vibration in one area of the universe can trigger a corresponding vibration in another part of the universe.

Science has determined that quantum travel happens along this connection, which further shows that everything is connected. That connection is not only at the substrate and physical level, but that connection is also what makes each of us part of the whole.

Other Connections

Since we are indeed connected by physical cords and quantum threads, it is then easy to see how what goes around comes around. This is the consequence that many in the East call karma. Karma and consequence are not just in the physical world as we saw in the connections between everything. They also exist in the quantum world.

That means it's not only the physical action that has an equal and opposite physical reaction, but intangible actions also have equal and opposite quantum reactions. How do these connections and consequences manifest? Well, they start out as intentions. When you have good intentions, you tend to have good things happen (forgive the use of the adjective "good"). When you have bad intentions, you see bad things happen.

Stoics, the people who want to understand the truth and control the things that happen to them, are highly conscious of the karma or the effect of the bad intentions that strike back in the quantum plane. Stoics, for this reason, keep their thoughts clear and sanitized. They do not like having ill-intentioned thoughts and do not like having thoughts that mean harm, are negative in any way, or deal with spite, envy, jealousy, or harm.

As you make your way through this book, you will start to get the impression that the mind of the Stoic is sterile and calm. It does not partake in any thought or chaos that will disrupt the life of a Stoic and detract it from seeking the truth and from being distracted in any way. Having bad thoughts during some downtime has the effect of changing the mood of the thinker and possibly bring ill effects in the physical world, which then has the consequence of derailing the other areas of the Stoic's life.

Thoughts are real to the Stoic. Most novices find that out very quickly. If you think of something hard enough with enough vibration, it will manifest in the physical world. It is how prayer and rituals work. Stoics read positive material to put themselves in the positive vibration and then do all they can to attract the positive energy that they use to find the truth.

Marcus Aurelius wrote in his personal journal, which was later published under the title Meditations, that "the happiness of your life depends on the qualities of your thoughts."

Killing

There is great misunderstanding about the issue of killing. The Bible clearly commands "Thou shall not kill." We go about thinking that it only applies to killing of humans, and we forget that killing an animal is also killing. Killing a bug is still killing. In fact, chopping down trees is still killing. We often think that killing is about the destruction of the victim. We think that we should not kill because it brings harm to the victim that is being killed. We feel pity for the victim, but it is not the victim who suffers.

In Stoicism, curbing the act of wanton killing is more about taking care of the aggressor than the victim. A person who is open to killing and who has killed for the sake of killing (not killing for the sake of sustenance) alters his own state of being. There is a form of aggression that comes to the person as he gets used to the act of killing and destruction.

Killing has a detrimental effect on the killer not to mention the loss to the community at large. It's also not just the killing of another human being that is the problem. Killing is also not a Stoic thing to do when it comes to killing animals (other than for food). Taking a life alters the trajectory of evil in the heart of the man who does the taking. It alters his being, his mind, and his existence.

Try going around and killing cats in the neighborhood (please do not do that; it's just a hypothetical) and you will see that it is you who suffers after some time. The more you kill, the more your energy changes. The Stoic does not kill because he is worried about the victim or the consequences of that act on the victim's family. He is protecting his own mind from the contamination and stain of taking a life.

Parallel to the issue of killing then comes the issue of eating animals and being vegan. The Stoic is not vegetarian because he does not want to kill animals. He may be vegetarian because he wants to enjoy the benefits of an agrarian diet. It has nothing to do with killing because killing for food to a Stoic is part of the circle of life. If not wanting to kill is the reason he is vegetarian, then that is inconsistent, as plants have life, too, and that is also killing when they are harvested.

It must be clear that a Stoic has no problem with killing for food or to save his life or the life of his family. But a Stoic's aversion to killing is so that he protects his mind from the consequences of guilt, pain, and committing an act that is irreversible and against nature.

To be certain that killing wantonly is against nature, look carefully at the balance of nature exhibits (save man) and you will notice that the full circle of life is done by the act of killing, but the killing is proportionate and purposeful. A lion kills a deer to feed its pride but not more than that. A deer could stroll past a lion that just finished his meal, and the lion would not do a thing. Nature only kills for advancing life.

The idea of killing what is necessary is the circle of life and does not go against nature and the construct of nature. For this reason, the Stoic does not consider the issue of harvesting or slaughtering when he picks his diet. Stoics, however, eat simple meals. They would rather keep their mind alert than gorge themselves with food and feel lax.

Stoics believe that death is the natural progression of life just as life is the natural progression of a pregnancy. When death comes, Stoics take it with an open heart. Although they are not looking forward to the event, they are also not going to feel bad about it since it is out of their control.

Stoics also believe that killing themselves, or committing suicide, is not the right thing to do, but in this case, there is an exception. Cato the Younger committed suicide when his principles were offended, and he knew that if he did not kill himself, Julius Caesar would demand his allegiance—something that went against the principles of Cato, who was a Stoic. According to Stoics, the only thing more important than one's life is your principles.

Pity vs. Empathy of a Stoic

The issue of killing, which in most minds is an issue of pity, does not apply to the Stoic. The Stoic is not one to engage in pity. He sees things as they are. If he sees an inequity and is able to help, he will. If he can't, he will not don the mask of pity and do nothing.

On the other hand, the Stoic has empathy, which has been misunderstood by most to be a deeper form of pity. It is not. Empathy is not sympathy, pity, or any other sort of internal bad feeling for another. Empathy is a whole different ball game and something that Stoics either naturally have or realize is part of the skill set they need to adopt rapidly.

Empathy is the string vibration that resonates within the person when they come into contact with another being—human or animal. That vibration can either indicate the person is happy or feeling sad or in a state of fear. Whatever is being transmitted from beyond the senses can be picked up by the person who practices empathy.

Judgment

Along with empathy comes another virtue that is practiced by the Stoic. He is not one to pass judgment or rely on prejudice to make up his mind about an issue. He sees each person as someone who is a novice regardless of whether or not they are on their path to being a Stoic or otherwise. Again, like the issue of killing, the issue of not holding anyone to judgment is a beneficial move for the Stoic, not the victim. When one does not have a prejudging mentality, that person is free to see things as they are and not through any distortion. We can never trust the notions of prejudice or the outcome of a proceeding that is tainted with judgment from the start. In fact, in the quest to find someone's culpability, even when there is evidence beyond the doubt that the person committed a crime, a Stoic is more inclined to offer forgiveness than to offer punishment.

In understanding the Stoic's nature of karma and consequences, we see that there are also various dimensions in the existence of all things—animate and inanimate. This fabric of the universe passes through all of us, and the Stoic is keenly aware of his unitary connection between all things. Science has just started to uncover this phenomenon and has labeled it the quantum phenomenon. The Stoics did not know the scientific angle of this, but they could observe it and been well aware of the effects for some time. In one's effort and journey from novice to Stoic, it is important to remember that all things are deeply connected. Empathy is just the vibration that travels through these connections. A person who is open to it, as a

Stoic is, is able to feel it and resonate with it. This is another reason why a Stoic needs the fortitude and strength to be able to have insight into things that would otherwise shake them to their core.

The realization that the novice should aspire to, which is something that happens at the end of many sessions of reflection and contemplation based on one's own life, is that everything is connected, and everything that he does even in the seemingly private corners of his mind will have a way to coming to reality if given the opportunity and time.

Chapter 4 - The Stoic's Character

The Stoic's character is not something that he starts off thinking about. In other words, he is not doing this to have better character. It just comes naturally, and his character starts to build as he starts to understand the world around him and improves the quality of his thoughts and actions.

The component of character that comes into the picture when one thinks about Stoicism is not driven by a set of rules and commandments. It is not even driven by the pride of being a Stoic. It's not as if you join a club and from there on you are sworn to walk and talk in a certain way. Stoicism is none of that. Stoics become the way they seem to be and take on an air of character and personality because of the way their mind evolves while they study the topics that are important to Stoicism.

It is fair to say that the character of a Stoic is one that is genuine and not a facade but the consequence of a mind that has been altered to understand the truth. The core principle and driving force of the Stoic is that he is in search of the truth and that he is the personification or at least tries to be the personification of truth.

The character of the world around us is one that is decidedly un-Stoic. It seeks to hide the truth when it is convenient. In fact, we are so preoccupied with how someone feels or how they feel about us that we twist the truth when they ask for it and it is inconvenient. How often have you heard someone tell a white lie in the face of being asked a question? This habit then grows. We think that speaking the truth will have a greater consequence on the person, and we try to shield them from the truth. All the while we undertake in deception that we feel is intended for the best.

The Stoic's character is part and parcel of his path and his pursuit. In fact, it is indistinguishable. Just as you are what you eat, so a Stoic is what he says and does. To a Stoic, engaging in half-truths, deliberate obfuscation, and outright lies is a state that is not worth living in. For this reason, the Stoic goes through great lengths to not put himself in a position that would require them to tell a lie or deal in untruths.

Because the truth is so important to his perspective of all things, including himself, the Stoic understands that if he leads a path that is unrighteous, he will eventually have to come to the point where he has to lie. Take, for instance, a man who is good in almost every way. Imagine further that he has a wife who is very accommodating. Now imagine that he has an affair outside his marriage and it happened in a manner that seemed to take place in slow motion. It was one step after the other that suddenly got too far, and the affair went into full bloom. Now his wife asks him about the affair, and to not hurt her feelings, he lies by denying it.

Putting aside the virtues or vices of having an extramarital affair, the lie that he would have to tell would have been enough for the Stoic to refrain from proceeding down that path. But if in the event he did go down that path and was indeed questioned by his wife, he would not hesitate to tell the truth.

Remembering that this book is not a book on the vices and virtues of married life, the illustration is designed to show three things.

(1) Lies are not tolerated by Stoics. If you claim to be a Stoic and you still engage in lies, then you may strip yourself of the fraternity of Stoicism. Lies demolish the path to Stoicism and reduces the mind to a state of fantasy and untruth.

(2) To show that because of the possibility of lying about his action in the future, the Stoic will forgo the action no matter how pleasurable or beneficial it may be at the moment. The value of telling the truth at some point protects him from making a mistake in the present.

(3) The need to think ahead. The desire of the Stoic to tell the truth requires that he see the chain of consequences that unfold in the natural course of things.

The three elements of the Stoic's incapability to lie sets up his character so that he is free from the obstacles that daily life brings. Dealing in the untruth is more than just telling a lie or speaking half-truths. It is a way of life that gets to the point where the person who practices it becomes incapable of knowing truth from fiction.

No matter how much a Stoic wants to embellish his point, he never crosses the line and falls into the reality of lies because that diminishes the truth that he is trying to deal in. When a person lies, it is more than his credibility at stake. It is his own familiarity with the truth.

The truth in the context of lies takes on two robes that you must seek out. The first is the lie that the person tells themselves. This is the untruth that they tell themselves in order to cope or feel better. This is also uncharacteristic of a Stoic.

The second robe that a liar wears is the robe of diminished consequence. That means that the person telling the lie thinks that it is not important. This happens when a person lies on a resume to get a job. We have come so far in this world that we think that lying is justified. A Stoic never sees a lie as something that is justified. No matter how small the lie or how large the consequence, lying will always lead to more calamity.

Not only is it the principle of the matter but in more cases than not a lie will also always have negative consequences down the road, and the Stoic is more concerned about unintended and negative consequences than almost any other person around him. Marcus Aurelius says in his writings, "To lie deliberately is to blaspheme - the liar commits deceit, and this injustice. And likewise to lie without realizing it. Because involuntary liar disrupts the harmony of nature - its order."

Transparency versus Lies

It is often not clear how to compare the two issues of transparency and lies. To most people, this is an easy issue, and it is one that does not even seem to be a question. If one has the choice to be opaque versus to lie, the person sees that opacity and lies are not the same thing, and so they will decline to lie but in reality dim the light on their own truth.

In no way does opacity reference the right of someone to personal or private information that could be used to bring about harm in any form. But transparency of your actions must always be practiced so that you can keep the forces of nature intact, and it serves as a guardrail so that you do not do anything that will cause you to be opaque in the future. The Stoic chooses silence of opacity and untruth unless his is certain that his silence could lead to the effective transmission of a lie.

A man's character is best determined by the actions and thoughts he has when no one is looking. By being transparent, not only does it show that he has nothing to hide, but it also gives him the confidence to hold his head up high without the fear of having to hide what or who he is. There is tremendous strength in that.

The issue of transparency by a Stoic in his community allows the prospering of the community and the strengthening of the Stoic himself. Being transparent is about the strength and benefit that come from it. If you have nothing to hide, you have nothing to be afraid of.

If you have nothing to be afraid of, then your strength can overflow into other areas. You will also gain the moral high ground. If you notice, many Stoics are pillars of their society and thought of very highly.

However, do not let this argument persuade you to dump all your private information onto the Internet and be free in your transparency online. This is not the same thing. If the Internet had been around during the time of Epictetus or Marcus Aurelius, then they, too, would have said to be transparent except when it comes to doing so in the blind, which is what you will be doing when you reveal information about yourself that could be used against you. No. Transparency is about being who you are, and that has two aspects to it that you need to consider.

The first aspect of that is the ability of being who you are is psychological in nature. If you can stand to be in your own skin, that brings about a kind of strength that is unparalleled. If you can't stand to be in your own skin, imagine the psychological nightmare that would result. To be a Stoic means that you are strong in many ways;

in fact, you are strong in all ways. It doesn't matter if you are skinny and have little musculature, but if your character is strong, you will win the day. But if you are opaque because you are fearful of what others think of you and about what you have done in the past, then you need to let the truth set you free, as the Bible so eloquently advises. So, too, does Epictetus and Seneca advocate for the telling of truth and the living of the same.

The second aspect of being yourself is about making your psyche immerse itself in truth. Once you are a person who is only interested in truth, not only are you going to act appropriately but you are also not going to be afraid of making a mistake because you will not have to carry the guilt of that mistake.

If you feel that you do not want others to know something about you, then you have to ask yourself why this is so. If the reason is that you are ashamed of it or you know in your heart that it was not a good thing, then you need to ask yourself why you are afraid of what others think of you.

The goal of being transparent is not just for the community but so that you can live a life of virtue. If you are ashamed of something, resolve it and then disregard what others think of you. A Stoic does not factor into his consideration the opinions of others.

Truth versus Virtue

The Stoic's view of truth is that it is not a virtue but an element of nature. The psychological aspect of truth is far-reaching. The mind is a habitual organ that does much of the things that it has to on a minute-to-minute basis based on habit. It wakes you up at a certain time of the day. It tells you when to smoke your first cigarette or your last before you turn in. It tells you when to hit the showers or head to the gym. The mind does what you train it to do. If you let it meander through the woods and pick up bad habits, then that is exactly what it is going to do. But even worse is that if you show it a swatch of the color blue and call it red, it will eventually label that blue swatch as red in your mind.

That is, of course, a simplistic illustration of the nature of the mind. The key is that you cannot during any part of your journey to Stoicism allow yourself to be put into a position that engages in anything but the truth. If you falter on this point, there is a chance that your mind starts to record the value and the meaning of truth. There is only one thing worse than a liar, and that is a liar who thinks that he is telling a necessary lie or that it is just true. Being a pathological liar is the risk you take when you engage in untruths. The opposite is when you start speaking the truth at all times without the risk of retribution. Then you start to streamline your actions so that you don't have to lie about it in the future. As Shakespeare says, "To thine own self be true."

Being transparent, telling the truth, and building the profile of recognizing the truth are all part of the bag of tools that the Stoic has in his arsenal. When he makes this into a matter of habit, then he is able to be free and direct his mind toward more important truths that he can uncover.

Strength

It would not be interesting if life were merely that simple. You can't just be open to the truth and not tell lies and the secrets of the world open up to you. Unfortunately, there is more to it than that. You also have to be strong because the truth is seldom easily accepted by you or those around you. It is much easier to accept a plausible lie than to accept the harsh and implausible truth.

It is also in the nature of most human minds to believe what they want to believe. To be able to deal in the truth, one must not create unnecessary expectations. This is the realm of the Stoic mind. He does not intend to deal in expectations or flights of fantasy because he is certain that it will alter his perception of the truth. But it is naive to think that the perception of the truth can't be influenced by the mistaken calculation or the momentary lapse in expectation. So the Stoic has the strength to alter what he has already committed to the mind as the truth if the evidence against it is fully supported.

The truth comes in more than one dimension. This is the truth of all things and all the things that are spoken and the things that are not always spoken. It is hard to find a true Stoic who deals in politics because he knows that politics, at least these days, is one of deception and half-truths. Stoics do not like being in the company of untruth, as it is contagious. This is one of Marcus Aurelius' greatest challenges. It vexed him in situations where truth and transparency came head-to-head with the matter of governing his empire.

But if Stoics are in it for the sake of doing a job, they would do so, and this is another reason they need strength. In today's world, being righteous takes tireless effort and perpetual vigilance. Strength provides both. You have to be strong to push forward, and you have to be strong to take the next blow.

The Stoic's strength goes both ways. He is strong so that he can push through the events he observes and extract the truth. He is also strong so that he can overcome the distractions of his primal self, which is one of the biggest distractions the mindful Stoic will ever face. All other distractions that occur externally can be walked away from, but the distractions internally are the ones that one has to live with and put a stop to. These present the greatest obstacles and the greatest opportunities.

Primal Distractions

The human body may be part of the divine framework, but it has been the result of a long line of evolutionary improvements and adaptations. We are still evolving and adapting as we speak. As you read this book, the neurons in your mind are preparing to alter the way they are arranged. In time, your thinking will change, and over the course of a lifetime you will have the choice on how you want that course to unfold.

Whatever your intentions, however noble and sincere, you will be faced with the internal distractions that will torment you and cause you grief. The best way to handle them is to understand them. The best way to understand them is to observe all the things that you think, say, and do. You cannot directly observe them. You have to do so indirectly.

These are the primal instincts that every person is born with. We have them as part of a repertoire of mechanisms that were designed to protect us, multiply us, bring us together, and spread the information among us. These primal instincts include the need to eat, to multiply the species, to mimic our neighbor, the fear of that which we do not understand, the formation of habits when it is pleasing to us, and a few others. All these become significant distractions to the Stoic who is trying to transition from the physical to the cerebral and then from the cerebral to the spiritual.

Each of us handles the primal instincts differently. The Stoic's job is to gradually understand himself and understand where these distractions are located and where they will take him when he gives in to those distractions.

Opinion Versus Truth

In most cases, it is easy for the Stoic or the novice on the path to being a Stoic to understand the meaning of the truth and to make the effort to identify it. However, there is another distinction, such as the one between opinion and truth. How does one treat opinion as compared with truth? Is opinion to be weighed in the same way? Is opinion to be based on the person who originated the opinion? As far as the Stoic is concerned, opinion is not the truth and should be taken as it is—hyperbole—until and unless sufficient evidence can be brought to bear on the matter and the truth of the matter emerges.

The Stoic is not interested in opinion that is over the top and has not evidence to swing it toward the side of truth. Opinion is one of the most biased of statements on any matter. It does, however, have its place in the discourse of exploration. But in the time of that exploration where no truth has been discovered. The Stoic understands this. Hypothesis and opinions are not the same either. Hypotheses are for the Stoic to test the truth of something that he guesses first and then gathers evidence for or against that hypotheses so that he may accept or discard it in the end. Opinion is not hypothesis.

Opinions are riddled with bias, prejudice, and approximations. It may not be the intention of the promoter of the opinion to mislead, but the intention is not the important aspect of the Stoic. It is the truth of the matter. Good intentions or otherwise, an opinion, by its nature, is not something the Stoic accepts in his discourse and evaluation.

This then comes back to the issue of strength. If the person is strong, he is able to set aside opinion in the absence of proof. Then again opinion with proof is fact, not opinion. So, in this case, the Stoic who is strong is able to set aside all opinion without being dissuaded from the truth or persuaded to accept an opinion.

The strength of mind is not one that is the same as the strength of arm or body. The strength of mind is one that is practiced and perfected over time. It is one that does not need too much effort and comes naturally or at least comes without hesitation.

Strength in deciding if something is the truth or engaging in facts that lead to the truth is a strength that exists in and of itself without the need to strenuously stand up to or against. It is a natural kind of strength.

Thus, the Stoic's character is the result of practice and the ardent pursuit of the truth. He needs to stay away from lies and opaque tendencies in his quest to seek the truth. The point is that if you don't deal enough in truth you will never be able to recognize it.

Chapter 5 - The Stoic Interpretation of God

The Stoic does not believe in God the way many believe in deities and personification of the Almighty. The Stoic realizes that God is a unifying force, and that is not the same as the God that the major religions of the world say it is. But at the same time, the Stoic does not discount their account of matters.

To believe in one's own religion or God and to be on the path of Stoicism is possible. In fact, it may make sense to many who practice religions, but it must be noted that the picture one sees in one's mind when the word "God" is uttered differs if the person is a Stoic or if the person is not.

That should not dissuade anyone from getting on the path of Stoicism. The ultimate definition of God is yours alone to make, and the Stoic philosophy merely points you to look at the nature of things and the nature within all things. How you see God after that point is up to you.

Many Stoics realize that God then is in all things of nature. Not just the birds and bugs or the rain and the forests, but in all tangible and intangible aspects of nature. Stoicism does not see God as a single being. In fact, he does not see God in the conventional sense of the word. The Stoic sees God as the sum of all things and the ultimate truth. There can be no inconsistency.

That takes some interpretation because on its own those with a mind that has been in a religious path for some time would interpret that statement in a way that is not intended. Stoics believe that God is the sum of all the things that you could possibly think of and all the things that you can't in all the forms and across all the universe. Everything from the tangible aspects of nature to the intangible ones are God. Everything that you can imagine and everything that you can't are God. The ultimate truth and the most profane lie are also God. There is nothing that you can think of, even evil, that is not a part of God.

This is the God of the Stoic. In undertaking his quest to understand all of nature and how nature works, the Stoic is undertaking the quest to find God. It is a large concept—too large for the untrained human mind to comprehend—but we must try. The journey to God is undertaken by understanding the nature of God, which is the nature of all things.

But there may be some who read this and do not believe in God. Understood. What is not believed is not God but the interpretation of God that has been offered by the various religions of the world. The kind of God that the Stoic believes in is not one that religions can contend with, but they are not evil in trying to describe God. The God they describe is designed to be understood by those they describe it to. To a Stoic, that is a brazenly insufficient explanation. Because, in part, the Stoic is aiming to transcend himself in the quest for the truth and the knowledge of God. If you tailor the message to suit him, then he remains as he is. No transcendence. This is unacceptable to the Stoic.

It is the key to understanding that God stretches from before the beginning of time and proceeds through the existence of space and whatever else there is in dimension. Our mind is not yet able to comprehend that, but the one thing for certain is that God is not interested in whether you honor your parents or you covet your neighbor's wife. The reason why that is important is not because God says so. It is important so that you do not face the consequences of those acts. It has nothing to do with God. The problem most people have with the Stoic's view of God is that they keep thinking that the God the Stoic envisions when the word is invoked takes on the appearance of a person—a biped with human features. A Stoic may not see it the same way. Even if he does, he realizes at the back of his mind that it is just a placeholder for something that encompasses so much more.

The Stoic's interpretation of God comes after a long period of observation and contemplation. It comes after countless hours of reflection and study. It is a pragmatic look at the idea of creation and the idea of continuation. The Stoic sees God as the past, present, and future all rolled into one. For all these nebulous descriptions of God, it then dawns on the Stoic that God is more than can be explained by books and a lifetime of contemplation.

To be a Stoic, it is required that the topic of God be approached with the least amount of prior study. All prior concepts and ideas should be discarded, and the question goes back to the beginning. It has to be an attempt at reintroducing the concept without the distractions of other interpretations.

The question then should be: "Is it possible to believe in a religion and still walk the path of the Stoic?" The answer is yes. The Stoic police aren't going to come and question you. There are no rules to any of this. You are something or you aren't. You decide to do something or you don't. There is no right or wrong way of doing something. Even if you are fooling yourself in the path you take, it is only you that will feel the consequences down the road—no one else.

Chapter 6 - The Core of Learning

One must learn from himself first above all else. That is the prime motivation and major artery of the Stoic's advance to illumination. No one can teach the novice until he decides he wants to be taught. That realization that he wants to be taught would have to come from his own quest and the questions that arise from it. Only at that point may he then seek out a teacher. Even then self-study and exploration are always the best teacher.

In the world we live in today, the distraction that makes up the bulk of living has caused the typical inhabitant of the human world to look at it from the perspective that everything is about materialistic consumption and trivial pursuits of satisfaction. That has led to widespread dissatisfaction and prolonged suffering across a wide swath of human consciousness.

Take, for instance, a homeless man who walks the city streets. He is blinded by the fact that the only way for him to survive is to eat the manufactured and processed foods that he has been so used to since the time, presumably, when he was a child. What he doesn't realize is that if he goes beyond the city limits and camps in the forest and finds the trees that offer shade and the shrubs that offer sustenance he would be able to survive. A little extreme, yet ironically simplistic, but the reason he doesn't do that is because he is addicted to the life that he was used to. He can't see beyond that.

That is the function of our inculcation. We are given a set of ideals and told that that is the minimum or the goals that we need to be a part of or adhere to. We are told as children that we need to eat three daily meals and snacks in between and that branded food and clothes are better than generic ones. So much so that we are short on resources, and the need to get bottom-shelf generic food items causes us to feel bad about ourselves. Why? Because of the learning that has been imposed on us—the inculcation of standards.

Only when one is exposed to hardships is one then brought face-to-face with the reality that maybe that is not the life that one should be living. Most of the original scholars of Stoicism came from the branch of philosophy that espouses asceticism. Now, that is an extreme, and no one even suggests that we should all give asceticism a try or make it a way of life, but it just goes to show that life is not what we have been told it is.

At the point of massive dissonance about the way we think we should live and the way our life turns out, we start to question everything, and we start to question the existence of Providence and the existence of religion. Some people then branch off to atheism and swear off the existence of God, whom they think should have protected them from the poverty, the loss, or the hardship they are facing. When they don't get an answer that they seek or can't find their way out of their troubles with a GPS, they start to despair. It is at this point that many ask so many questions, but most often those questions are of the wrong kind.

In time, they begin to realize that maybe it is the question that is wrong, and then they start to ask the right questions at which point they become a novice in search of the truth. This is the first step to learning, which is not the collation of data and memorization of facts. Learning is the process of understanding the truth of all things beginning with the most fundamental areas of existence.

As a philosophy, Stoicism is the map that allows someone to frame the questions that they conjure in the depth of depression or sadness or at the heights of intellectual curiosity. Either way it starts from within, not without.

It is not necessary for the novice to engage a teacher until he gets to the point that the stream of questions is so voluminous that his own contemplation exercises are unable to unearth the answers that he seeks.

The Stoic's path to learning is one that is different from what most are used to or aware of. It is easy to fall into the trap that we only learn from a guru or a teacher. The Stoic knows that the only true teacher in all things is life itself, but to learn from this teacher, one must go beyond the sensory endowments one is given to navigate the physical world and tap into the intellectual endowments that is part of everyone's profile.

One cannot be recruited, proselytized, or coerced into embracing the philosophy and thinking of a Stoic. Not only is that counterproductive, but it is also ineffectual and inconsistent with the foundations of Stoicism.

The human psyche is developed by its surroundings, which is a multidimensional proposition. It is not just a handful of elements or situations that make it so. It is a complex weave of interrelated and seemingly unrelated assets found in the universe. From gravity to climate to surroundings. After all, one cannot make cacti thrive in the Arctic just as one cannot see icebergs in tropical waters.

Even though those examples point to physical objects, they represent the truism that one is the sum of his environment, and that environment includes time and other intangible phenomena. Just because you drop an iceberg into the middle of the Sahara does not mean it instantly ceases to exist. It will take time to melt, wet the sand,

and then evaporate into the air and disappear. The element of time is always a part of the equation in a Stoic's calculus yet mostly unseen by any of the forces or senses we are endowed with.

This is the aspect that typically triggers the mind to ask questions. It is those series of questions that eventually asks the question "Who am I?" that begins the quest for greater answers. Each Stoic begins his path from a different point, but he then traces that path to a common destination. Just as the saying in the classical world that "All roads lead to Rome" so, too, in the human journey we find that all roads lead to Truth. Truth is not the absence of a lie. Truth is not the expounding of one set of facts while denying another. Truth is significantly more than that, and it takes active participation and serious reflection to ascertain it. That is the journey of the novice and the quest of the Stoic.

Very close to the original question of Who Am I? comes the question What is Truth? —truth is not a point of data or the accuracy of a narrative. It is a state of being that you occupy when you reach the end of your journey as a Stoic. In other words, the Stoic is not the person who finally has reached the truth but rather someone who has gotten on the path to seek Truth. A Stoic adjusts his mental, physical, psychological, and spiritual frequency to place him on the path so that he trains his corporeal existence to find the Truth that he seeks.

To become a Stoic is to say that one is on the path to understanding and living the Truth. It is not an academic or a philosophical exercise. It is a practice that allows one to learn about himself and to learn about the universe in a way that is beyond the material sciences that are taught in school. Once that Truth appears on the horizon, the Stoic becomes more in tune with what the Truth is and takes on a very different state from that he first took as a novice.

No one can teach the novice to be a Stoic. They can list what it looks like to be a practicing Stoic. They can make a laundry list of attributes and rules, but they will never be able to dye the fabric of the person with the truth that defines the

Stoic. Stoicism comes from harmonizing the Self with the Truth that is all around.

For that reason, Stoicism is mostly about reflection, contemplation, and surrender than it is about memorizing rules, commandments, and dogma. Stoics are more about all-encompassing change than they are about isolated changes in thought, word, and deed. Stoics are about the whole picture rather than the keyhole view of something much larger.

Step Two

If you are wondering where Step One is, you would need to go back and read the start of the chapter. Step One is about coming up with the question that would put you on the path to Stoicism. It is about feeling the pain of being in the wrong state of existence and then asking the question about where you should be.

Step One is about truly asking yourself the question "Who am I?" And not just mouthing the question but really seeking to find the answer. When you get to that point, then you are at Step One. Once you can feel that question resonate so loudly in you and you can't find the answer—and you shouldn't. If you already know the answer, then it's only what you think. Keep going because you don't yet know the question of "Who am I?"

Step One should make you feel lost. It should suddenly occur to you that you have no idea who the I, in Who am I?, is. Only then will the part of you that wants the answer wake up. Until you get to that point, Stoicism or any other philosophy is not going to help you in any meaningful way. You do not become a Stoic before understanding who you are or even asking that question.

Many people are arrogant enough to answer that question with inane answers, such as "I am a Banker" or "I am a lawyer" or "I am a doctor." Well, that is great. We have now determined what you do to make a living, but that is not who you are. If your answer to the Step One question is that you are a lawyer, doctor, salesman, driver, or something that describes what you go out and do on a daily basis to bring back the bacon, then you are not even close to answering the point in Step One.

The question in Step One is the greatest stumbling block to getting started on your path to becoming a Stoic. Once you do get past Step One, then in Step Two the process of learning begins. The process of learning here is to discover who you are beneath. Step Two can only begin when you realize you do not know who you are because you have shed the identities that have been bestowed upon you by the things you have done in your life. You are not a graduate or a mayor. You are not a father or a daughter. You are not any of those labels, but who then are you? That is the point of Step Two.

The Stoic is in constant search for that answer. You may ask what does asking that question and then finding the answer have to do with the truth and Stoicism. If that is the question, then it is one that can be answered so that you can get under way in your quest to be a Stoic. By the way, once you have practiced the path of the Stoic and you can adequately refer to yourself as a Stoic, even that does not answer the question "Who am I?"

To reiterate, learning the principles that define Stoicism is merely a framework that gives you the picture to begin understanding the answer. Think of it this way: Stoicism is like the 3D goggles that you wear when you walk into the theater to watch a 3D movie. Until you put them on, whatever is projected on the screen remains hazy and out of focus. Once you put on the goggles, the picture comes into focus, and you experience the movie. In the same way, Stoicism is the goggles that you wear, while the movie is the life around you. The truth is what you realize after you order the movie days after it is done. If you just walk out of that movie content with the giggles and the tears that the movie elicited but you failed to see the point of the movie or the greater story at play, then you have missed the point still.

Stoicism is the goggles that you need to put on and look around so that you can see things as you should to make the Truth come into focus. To extend the analogy, you must realize that you can't walk around wearing these 3D goggles before you decide to go out and watch the movie. The goggles will be of no use, and in fact it will obscure your way of life, and you will be bumping into things, and things will begin to actually make less sense.

If you are not ready to find out the answer to the simple question of Who am I? and what is the truth, then the notion of understanding Stoicism is a quaint, albeit useless one.

There is a long history to Stoicism that has been covered in previous books. These books take it deeper, and you should read them to be able to get a better idea of the content and the point of this message.

Once you have posed the questions and they resonate at a visceral level and you want to see the truth of all things and understand yourself in the context of that truth, you are on your way. Stoicism will not provide the answer to those questions, but it will give you the tools to find the answer. If you find a map that needs special glasses to see it in order to find the treasure, you need to use the glasses to see the treasure map, and that will tell you the path you need to take. You still have to take the path and walk through its challenges.

Once you do that and after years of following the map, you find the end of the line and the treasure of Truth awaiting your arrival. That journey is the life you lead based on the map that you follow.

Chapter 7 - The Path to Progress

Stoicism is all about progress. Progress does not mean that you are able to afford the best clothes and the finest food. Progress is about movement in the right direction. Nothing happens overnight. It is like yogurt and cheese. You have to let the process take its time and be patient while you wait. A Stoic understands that all things have their own nature, and you have to allow for that nature to take place.

Nature is not the plants and trees that grow around you. That is not the nature we are referring to here. The nature here is the sequence of events and the time it takes for things to happen. If you use cement to hold bricks in a wall together, you have to give it time to set. That time is the nature of the cement. If you plant a seed, you need to give the seed time to germinate. That time is its nature. If you throw a ball toward a wall at a certain speed and trajectory, it will take a certain amount of time for it to come back to you. That is nature. You have to give nature its turn in all actions. If you throw the ball to the wall and are in a hurry to catch the return, you will not be successful.

This is the secret to a Stoic's success. He understands the nature of progress. You cannot rush it. You have to do your best and then wait for nature to take its course. Above all else, a Stoic is a person who understands the harmony and frequency of things around him. It takes years of observation and patience to adopt the nature of things, and then they will be able to master the way things unfold around them.

When you practice Stoicism, it is not going to be in a void where what you do for a living or how you raise your family will be separate and unrelated to your life as a Stoic. Everything in life is connected just as every action has a consequence. It is thereby reasonable to think that every action has consequences that are sometimes unintended.

Stoics account for this, but since when one starts out it is not easy to predict, you can only perfect this with experience and learning from mistakes. To a Stoic, life and the mistakes that one makes in life are the prime teachers in all things. That is why, unlike other philosophies and religions, there is no need for a master or a guru. There is only observation.

Progress is made by staying true to the objective and not having any form of expectations. The only image that a Stoic carries in any attempt at a task a Stoic undertakes is the outcome of that task and the achievement of that goal. Everything at that moment is not relevant and thus not worth paying attention to. That way a small measure of progress is made in one unit of time that will then become the basis of the next task. Even though it may seem slow, it is done with meticulous attention paid to only one thing—the attention at hand.

The same applies to the words that the Stoic reads. It goes to the conversation the Stoic has. Nothing the Stoic does is done without the element of progress percolating at the back of his mind. Many wonder why Stoics are so bent on success and achievement. They wonder if it is the wrong pursuit and the folly of the hungry. It is neither.

Stoics understand that measurable progress is the path to greater achievements, which are the measure of one's life. Sitting in meditation for the sake of meditation does not yield anything. Sitting in meditation so that one's mind is sharper for the next task they are about to undertake makes all the difference.

A Stoic sees the perfection of God in all things. While he is not a holy man nor does he propose to be, he understands that there is greater hand at work that is more than his existence. That power would continue after his present form is brought to its natural end, and that force existed before his present form was created. The Stoic knows this and understands that it is what it is. Because he understands that power is great and that he would never exist without it, he is conscious of that power and venerates it so that he does not run afoul of its trajectory.

It's like standing at the side of the highway while hundreds of cars speed past you on the curb. Would you even consider running across the highway in front of these fast-moving vehicles? No, you will observe them but not challenge them by placing yourself in their path. This is the same relationship that the Stoic has with his God. He does not want to run in opposition or across his God's path and would rather mind his own business seeking his own enlightenment keeping in mind that the consequences of his actions do not inadvertently put him at odds with the nature of that God.

So then, how does God, nature, and progress come together in the mind of a Stoic?

These three elements are the foundation of the Stoic's purpose and mind-set. Not all Stoics are found to be philosophers or generals. They go about their daily life being doctors and lawyers. How they put food on the table does not have much to do with the nature of the virtues, but many times their path of success and the method by which they secure shelter and clothe and feed themselves are one and the same.

Stoics do not go to a meeting once a week, promise to follow certain virtues, and then come home and spend the other six days of the week doing the exact opposite. Stoics are not bestowed the name. They are either Stoics or not. They are not bestowed the titles by any governing body or organization.

The fabric of the Stoic persists in all forms of his responsibility and daily schedule. He is a Stoic in words and deeds while he is in meditation, and he is a Stoic when he is at his shop selling his wares. He is a Stoic at school, and he is a Stoic when he is out having coffee with his friends. A Stoic is dyed in the wool and not projected onto a canvas.

The Stoic's progress is inextricably tied to the ideals and virtues of his philosophy. He does not bend the truth so that he can make an extra dollar in his endeavors, and he does not skimp on the ingredients he puts into his product. He is more concerned about what he sees as just and equitable.

Equity is the cornerstone of the Stoic's progress. It is not the monetary gain at the expense of someone's loss that determines the progress of a Stoic. It is more the opposite. The Stoic understands that there must be equity in all actions and transactions. In the event the Stoic is uncertain about his actions, he looks at equity in the relationship, and if he finds that there is inequity as part of the relationship, he realizes that it needs to be addressed. This goes both ways. A Stoic is just as unaccommodating with inequities that benefit the other person as he is with inequities that benefit himself. The question is never about who benefits past the point of equity. It is about whether or not inequity exists.

The Stoic understands that progress is a function of equity. Whenever there is equity, greater progress can be made across a wider array of circumstances. In today's context, equity manifests in reputation, profit, and goes on to be a long-term benefit that results in a better yield than a one-off supernormal profit in a transaction that results in dire inequities to the other party.

The next element of progress is about mistakes. A Stoic seeks to make mistakes as much as a child seeks to try to walk. The child knows that he has no clue how to balance himself while his legs are trying to reach forward, so the best way to do it is to try. Failure just means that particular way of doing something does not work, and so the Stoic learns a number of things from just one instance of failure.

Obstacles

The best way to learn something is to take the path with the most obstacles. This does not mean that you take the path heading east just so that you can go west. It is not about taking the unnecessarily long way to the destination or the unnecessarily steep path to the top. But to the Stoic, the obstacle is the way.

It may seem that the path of least resistance would be the smarter way of doing things, but it never is. The path with the least number of obstacles is usually the wrong path that would lead to ruin and disaster. After many trials and errors, the Stoic finds this out. He also finds that out of ten times it may be possible that two or three times the easier path may reach a profitable conclusion, but the other seven times the harder path always does, and the level of success is much higher and shared with fewer competitors. For that reason, it becomes commonplace to see that Stoics always take the path filled with obstacles.

There are many ways of looking at it, but one way should drive your decision to always take the path of hindrance. It is the path less traveled but with the most opportunities. If you are only willing to reach for low-hanging fruit, you have to contend with all those who came before you or are standing next to you and who are just investing little to get what they want. But the moment you decide that you are going to reach for the fruit that is higher up in the tree, you will find that not many are willing to make the climb, and you will find a wider selection of fruit and a higher number of fruits on the higher branches.

Taking the path that has the most obstacles does one other thing for you. It gives you better equity for the same amount of time spent. In other words, you get better outcomes for the same amount of time spent on the road that has no obstacles. The only difference is that you would have to put in the effort and do it for a longer period of time.

Stoics are by no means masochists. They are not doing the extra work for the same return. That is not what taking the obstacle-filled road means. Doing more work for lesser return is inequitable, and this is not something that a Stoic would even consider. Granted, the more one practices taking the path of obstacles, the greater the returns would be, and that means the initial steps would render the effort less profitable, but that is the price you pay to learn the ropes.

Silence in General

The final element of progress is that is must be conducted in silence. Silence is about the direction of effort and focus. The more one is busy talking, the more he is unable to do what he has to do. The more he is busy talking, the less his mind will engage in the endeavor, and he will lose out on any opportunity to learn from his mistakes and any possibility of future progress.

Without silence one cannot find progress. The nature of silence is one that escapes most people, and it is the reason behind the misunderstanding of the Stoic's demeanor.

Silence is the core of all things. The Stoic sees silence in two ways.

The first perspective of silence is that it allows them time to evaluate and understand. It gives them the focus to reflect and go deeper in their quest of understanding.

The second perspective of silence is to be able to rein in the mind that is chaotic. The Zen Buddhists call this the monkey mind. Once the monkey mind is unleashed, it takes on a life of its own and continuously derails all rational thought. The Stoic is always looking to remain balanced in a rational manner, and the random thoughts of the monkey mind distracts from this.

By practicing silence in all scenarios, there is a momentum of silence that is created, but that silence is not the silence of the mind or the lack of any real thinking or contemplation. The Stoic is constantly in an alert state even if he is not speaking or thinking of many things at once. This is the reason why he is always calm and collected.

The silence of the lips and the silence in meditation are not always the same thing. The silence of the lips is tasked for a different purpose than the silence that is involved for the purpose of reflection and then for the purpose of meditation. The silence invoked during meditation is significantly different from the silence invoked during contemplation.

The Stoic finds the divine in the silence that he is able to invoke. In the last chapter, there is a little bit more about how the Stoic looks for the divine and the thoughts he has on the subject, but for now the precursors to that conversation are found in the way the Stoic approaches silence.

There are three steps in silence. The first step is the step of physical silence. In physical silence, one just stays quiet and allows others to talk or sits back and observes the world around him. It is the mechanical silence that allows the senses to invoke input. The mind may be in contemplation or in active creation of things. It is only the lips that are silent.

The second step in silence is when the lips remain silent, but the mind is actively listening to the incoming information. The mind is not cogitating or preparing a response. In this case, the mind and the lips are silent.

The third step is the silence of the mind and the lips, but this time it is not about the input of external stimuli or information. It is about the silencing of the mind. This is the meditation that the Stoic embraces. In Stoic meditation, there is no thought or conversation. This kind of silence is the anticipation for inspiration and subconscious communication. It is a deep and productive use of silence.

Silence in meditation is when the Stoic stops all external communication and retreats into his own space and then shuts down the cogitative process of the mind so that the subconscious can inspire him in the direction that needs advancement.

Silence in Reflection

The kind of silence that is required in reflection is not the same as that in meditation. In meditation, there is a deep silence, but in reflection there is an external silence and the silence of unnecessary thoughts. Stoics believe in something that can be referred to as the Momentum of Thought. The longer you can focus, the more momentum you can build and the more you can contemplate in a given amount of time. In other words, ten minutes of focus that is done continuously is worth a lot more contemplative power than a minute of contemplation done ten times with a break between each time. For this reason, Stoics plan their contemplation over long periods of uninterrupted silence and when they are absolutely alone.

Reflection is not the same as contemplation. Reflection is specifically conducted to analyze one's own actions and history. Contemplation is the cogitation of matters that need analysis and understanding.

Reflection is designed to match action of the self to consequences that happen externally. It's like hitting the tennis ball and then observing its return trajectory and then associating the action to the reaction. This is an important aspect of reflection and increases the effectiveness of the Stoic's actions and focuses his thoughts.

A Stoic reflects separately from his meditation, and he reflects on a daily basis. Reflection is usually done in the privacy of his own peace without any possibility of interruption. A solid hour of silence in reflection will yield amazing results in just a month if done consistently and daily. The momentum of the action will create an internal realignment of the mind's schedule and the mind's involvement. In time, as the mind learns to use this tool to better its choices and understanding of the self, it will look forward to the time when the reflection is done. The best time for this reflective period is before turning in for the night.

From a neuroscientific point of view, the timing of reflection just before sleep at night allows the brain to rearrange the neurons that were involved during the reflection and rewire the way the brain thinks. In time, the brain becomes better because of it and turns the Stoic into a supercharged achiever.

Silence in Contemplation

This silence is the same as the silence for reflection except the purpose and the objective are different. In contemplation, you analyze the events and the reactions. In contemplation, you analyze the what-ifs. You contemplate the larger questions. You think about what you read about the larger questions of life and the bigger picture that you do not normally get to visit during the course of the day. It is also a time that you contemplate your actions that have not yet happened.

The silence is as specific as the other kinds of silence. In the mode of contemplation, you have no time for their chatter and worry. Whatever is going on in your life that is beyond your mind at the time of the silence is not your concern at that point. There is no problem so serious that it has to invade this period of contemplation. Make this a habit as all Stoics do and you will see that within the same month there will be a difference in the manner of contemplation, and you will also see a more powerful ability to visualize and contemplate the larger questions. This is the part that has direct consequence on the life you live and the contributions that you make. For those who have a career, this is the time that you take to understand the career that you have and the best way to advance that.

Chapter 8 - Stoic Thought Process

The Stoic thought process is easy to inculcate but hard to understand. You could easily follow an algorithm-like set of steps and then just plug in the key elements of the different issues you are facing and regurgitate solutions to any given situation. That is certainly one way of doing things, but that would not be the true Stoic way.

In other situations, you could have rules that are codified to tell you what you must or must not do in any given situation, and that saves you the effort of thinking of being mindful of your actions. Then there are times when one's state of existence is at odds with the philosophy or rules that have been applied to him. That creates more problems and strife. Imagine being vegan (nothing against vegans) in a land where only green grass and cows exist. On the other hand, imagine being strictly carnivorous in a land that has only fauna and flora with no critters as far as the eyes can see or the legs could walk.

These dogmas and tenets create an untenable position for both of these situations and instead of bringing peace, bestow stress and discord. However, a Stoic is not one of those people who turns around and feels stressed by the situation that is around him because he does two things. He first makes best use of the environment around him. If he needs to be a hunter to be able to survive, that's what he does. He understands that the universe wants him to survive above all else, and it is in that fight to survive that all life thrives.

Charles Darwin found two species of tortoise on two close-by is as in the Galapagos. Both had different neck structures. One could reach above to harvest the leaves and twigs of the short trees, but the other could not. He was curious why there was a difference, and then he found that the turtle that could lift his head up lived on an island that had abundant trees with low branches but had a sparse distribution of shrubs. On the island where the other turtle was located—the one that could not lift its head up too high—there were only ground shrubs. It turns out that both tortoises had adapted perfectly to their surroundings.

Imagine if there were a Tortoise dogma that said that tortoises could only eat what was at ground level and not from trees. What would have happened to the tortoise population at the second island where there were only low trees and no shrubs? If they had followed the dogma and the commandments, they would have eventually perished.

Stoics realize that their first rule is that they have to survive, so they are supposed to do whatever they can to live. Whether they have to eat sheep or snake, pheasant, or critter is not the point. There are no limitations. They have to do whatever is necessary to survive. If they have to hunt boars and kill them, so be it. They will do it without guilt but with gratitude. On the other hand, just because they have the ability to hunt the boar, does not mean that they would make it into a sport and hunt the best and leave it as carrion. That balance is the mind-set of the Stoic.

The Stoic's thought process is personal and bespoke. It is built from one's own experience, and it should take into account the kinds of experiences the individual has. It should not be a boilerplate response to what someone else might have experienced and things that it would work on another. It almost always would not. A Stoic who lives in the current generation is not required to eat what Marcus Aurelius ate, sleep the way Chrissipus slept, or work as a slave the way Epictetus did. He merely has to do what is necessary to survive in today's environment.

The necessary condition, however, to understanding the Stoic way of life and to love it is not to follow the actions blindly but to follow the mind-set and create an action plan accordingly. That mind-set is the Stoic Thought Process that this chapter is about. It is something that you have to adapt over the course of your life and make it your own.

What you have to do, however, is follow a step-by-step plan to build your own Stoic thought process so that the resulting pattern is one that meshes well with your mental patterns yet delivers a Stoic state of being to your routines and decision-making process.

With enough practice, you will find that you will end up being able to think like a Stoic on the fly compared to when you first start off, where you may lean on your past fears and anxieties in your decision-making process.

Contemplation Before the Fact

A Stoic is not an automaton, which means that contrary to erroneous and widespread belief that he has predetermined responses to every situation, the Stoic is in full focus and in full control of his faculties at all times because he knows himself well.

This is the mark of the Stoic. Not only does the Stoic conquer himself, but he is also able to contemplate on the nature of things and how they work so that his actions in response to an event are based on the nature of things and not the impulse to protect his sensitivities and fears.

For instance, if a Stoic understands that an aggressive dog is barking at him because the dog himself is threatened or protecting his turf, then the Stoic is not going to allow his own fear to get the better of him. He understands that all things have their nature, and as long as you do not go against that nature whatever situation that is currently front and center can be tempered and prevented from escalating beyond control.

This comes from the contemplation that all Stoics take part in. Some may call it reflection, some may call it meditation (although it is not meditation), and some may call it thinking. Whatever you want to call it is fine. We call it contemplation before the fact. That means you are thinking about things before they are in front of you and pressing you for a response.

Above all else when you get started on your path to Stoicism, you should look at your own life and understand the way you see things and the way you react to things. This is your ground zero. From here all things can change, and all things can stay the same if you so desire. The power to control what happens next is in the hands of the Stoic because he chooses to take control of where and when he places his next step or utters his next word.

Contemplation Before the Fact needs the art of observation. The art of observation is the ability to observe things without judging and without feeling. In this case, feeling is the emotional response that overpowers the cerebral response. It is the phenomenon that freezes a deer in the headlights and brings about its demise. A Stoic is detached from his emotions so that he can apply logic and reasoning to his observations and extract from them the nature of the event or object at hand. This is the core of a Stoic's powers. Once he can attract the nature of each individual event and element, he is able to protect them and predict the course of future events to a high degree of certainty.

Take, for instance, the father of a young child. The father knows to a high degree of certainty that the child is going to respond in a particular way in a particular situation. He often does not judge his child because he knows this child well and is ready for the child's response.

In the same way the father knows the reasons of the child because he understands that child's particular nature, all Stoics understand the nature of things because they have chosen to observe and understand all things.

A Stoic's silence is not one of aloof arrogance. It is one of constant study. The Stoic is busy assimilating the nature of all that surrounds him and linking that new information to the old and updating his understanding of all things. The more the Stoic understands the nature of things, the more he is able to predict the outcome of any situation, and as this improves so does his predictive accuracy over a wide scope of his environment. When a scientist studies water and finds out that every time he heats water it boils at exactly 100 degrees Celsius, he can predict that it will boil at 100 degrees Celsius the next time he places a pot on the stove. The same happens in all areas of nature.

Now imagine if the Stoic goes to Mars where there is a different boiling point for water and he sticks to dogma that water boils at 100 degrees. He will soon be disappointed. A Stoic is, however, not used to being disappointed because he does not have expectations. He understands that dogma that water must boil at 100 degrees must be altered according to the situation that is prevailing.

In the same way, life changes in different circumstances and when different forces are applied to the same situation. Man's nature is no different. It is still nature, and it will still follow the path that is determined by the forces that are applied to it. A Stoic knows that a man will react in a certain way if he is placed in a certain set of forces acting on him. If those forces are changed, the man will change his actions. For this reason, Stoics look to the forces and not the man to understand what his next action is going to be.

To be able to do this, he is constantly contemplating before the fact. He is looking at all forces and understanding how the forces determine the action and the reaction. Your question then is to apply things to yourself. How do you take the forces around you to see how you react to things that happen around you? A Stoic breaks this down even further. He looks at who he is and the forces that exist around him. The forces that exist around you are not limited to the objects that are there. Forces are not just material objects but also invisible forces, such as gravity and magnetism. When a charming girl walks into the room, the invisible force she has on some of the men in the room that makes them act like total imbeciles is well documented. To think that it won't happen is to be blind to the invisible forces that exist around us.

The point is that observation yields interesting results that most people do not always realize are present. There are two forces in the external, and there are two forces in the internal. The forces in the external are the forces that exist outside the Stoic's self. These are divided into objects and the invisible forces that exist. Think about it this way. Washington, D.C. was designed in such a way as to keep visiting dignitaries in awe of the capital city when they arrive. The White House is also built in such a way that it can be extremely intimidating to foreign dignitaries when they arrive. These are visible objects and invisible forces that are designed to alter the reaction of the people who enter it and to keep the advantage for the home team. This is just an illustration to make the point that there are two forces to be aware of when creating an observational framework.

An observations framework is a conceptual notion that allows you to decompose all that you observe. What we say as visible and invisible forces are merely this: anything that you can see, hear, smell, touch, and taste is observable. Anything that you can't use your five senses to detect is sometimes considered unobservable. To be able to observe that which cannot be detected by the five senses has to be observed by the mind.

You cannot observe the intention of a person by using your five senses, but you can figure it out. You can't see gravity that the earth exerts on all things, but you can figure that there is a force that pulls things.

So the Stoic is able to understand that he has to bring his mind to bear on all things that he is exposed to. The beauty of doing this is that once the mind comes online then it is able to see more than just the things that exist as objects and forces but also able to see in a deeper dimension.

For the ability to Contemplate Before the Fact to be effective, you first have to know yourself. It is not important at this point that you change yourself but more important that you know who you are and how you react to all things big and small.

To know thyself, as the Romans would advise, you have to spend time observing your own actions. To observe your own actions, it would be difficult to do that in reality without any practice, so you are going to have to start observing yourself after the fact. That means you should spend time at the end of each day looking back at your actions and the way your actions reverberated through the universe.

There are two elements to this action of observing yourself. The first is to understand why you responded the way you did to any situation. The second is to see how your response fell on the world around you. For instance, if you hit a drum, what did the drum do. In this case, of course, it made a loud noise.

In the same way, your framework for understanding yourself is done by looking at the reason you reacted in the way that you did. Sometimes this is not as clear as we think it is. It is not uncommon for people to think that they react intentionally and predictably to a particular situation, but that is never the absolute case. People react in a way that seem unpredictable because there is a lag in the way we process the preceding event, and that lag in processing causes the emotion from that event to overflow in the subsequent event however unrelated it may be.

For instance, if you were to get a really severe tongue-lashing from your superior at work just before quitting time, how would your drive home work out? It would be one where you are in a bad and brooding mood. In no way is the drive causing you to feel bad or feel uncomfortable. It was the preceding event that overflowed into the present situation. On a normal day, if someone cut you off in traffic, you might let it go, but on this day, you might have a few choice words and hand gestures to signal your state of existence at that point.

When you observe yourself at the end of the day, you should then be able to dissect the events and then decompose them of the relevant threads so that you understand how your behavior and your choices are dictated by things that you are not yet in control of.

Observing yourself takes practice to be able to yield a proper result. There is one more layer that a Stoic goes through before he is confident in this ability to evaluate his actions and the thought process that resulted in those actions.

He looks back at similar instances and understands how he acted to see if there is a common thread of response in the way he sees things or responds to them. The last time he got into an argument with his boss did he behave to unrelated events in the same way? If there is correlation, then he has to ask himself how that happens. But for now, until that is resolved, he should have a temporary rule that the next time he gets into a shouting match with his superior that maybe he should take a walk in the park or take a cab home instead or otherwise just be alone until he is in a mental state to be able to handle other people around him.

This is one way to know yourself—by looking at your past actions and then comparing them to similar actions that you have faced in the past. There were two things that we said you must be aware of. The first was the person in the case you and how you react and the second was to look at how your reaction was perceived by the rest of the world.

This second issue is the counterbalance to the first issue. The first issue was to determine how you saw the incoming event, and the second issue is your ability to look at the outgoing event. In the outgoing event, you need to look at how it was taken by the people that it fell on.

This will allow you to be able to tune your response for better effect in the future. So, for instance, if someone cut you off at the checkout counter at the grocery store while you were in a foul mood from some preceding event, then the person who cut you off might have been a mother with a young child who was buying one item and who was otherwise in a hurry. (I am not condoning the jumping of lines at the checkout counter; it is merely to say that she had a really good reason.) This reason may have been obvious to everyone else except you because you were off your game. On any given day, you may have gladly allowed her to jump the line, but today you were just not in the right frame to do it. In your contemplation, you realize that event would not a bad one, but it is not that event that you need to be focusing on. What you have to do is look at the effect that it had on all those around you.

This is a very simplistic illustration, but the point remains that you need to look at how your action falls on those around you. It's like a tennis player who receives a curve ball and plans on returning the ball to the base line. Once the player makes the hit, he has to observe whether that hit landed on the base line or wherever it landed, and then in that reflection he can make changes to determine what he has to do to get what he wants. The idea of reflection is to see if the intended response had the intended effect.

Most people have one of two effects. Only a small percentage of reactions are even the appropriate ones. The two reactions that are not the appropriate ones are the reactions that are not well thought of or the stunned and frustrated silence that arises from not knowing what to do.

Those who do not reflect on the nature of things and understand themselves would most likely react poorly because they do not know what they want from the reaction. Life is too short and energy is too expensive to waste it on a move that will not yield the benefit that you can carry into the future.

The more you are able to do this, the more you will gradually become tuned to the way the nature of incoming stimuli and outgoing responses work, and then you can use that to understand how to benefit from it. None of this is about changing to become a better person. The idea of responding just so that you can take out your frustrations is never a good idea and has nothing to do with becoming a better person.

Once you observe how you react and how others feel at your reaction, then you start to see how to react in a way that gets you what you want. But none of this can happen without being able to observe with the mind.

The last thing that you have to keep in mind is that you should never contemplate the actions, unless it is now a life or death consequence, in the moment. Thinking about whether or not to do something is always a good thing, but that is not what we are referring to when we say do not contemplate in real time. Your frame of mind, your emotions, and your state preclude you from being able to accurately and effectively analyze and contemplate any event in real time and will only serve to tie your mind up in knots. Thinking about how to respond is another matter. That just applies your thinking to what you should do. It is not analyzing the effects and the nature of things. You should never analyze the nature of things in real time. Leave that for your contemplation sessions, which should usually happen at the end of the day.

Stoics are not angry people for this reason because in time they learn that anger never gets them what they want, and it is a huge waste of energy and time. Anger is only the energy that is conjured during moments of frustration and lack of clear direction in where to go and what to do next. If you are a person who usually flies off the handle at a moment's notice, it is likely then that the reason is that you do not know how to handle the situation because you do not know the nature of things before you, and you do not know how to respond.

Observe with the Mind

A Stoic observes with his mind. He cannot observe with his senses because they will deceive him. The mind is the only tool that can observe anything, and it is the mind that can be altered to change the filter of observation so that the proper result is extracted from the experience.

Stoics spend more than a quarter of their life observing the nature around them. This is the nature that is intangible. They see things that the eyes can't see. The mind is the only thing that is able to discern the intangible qualities of all the things around you. You can't see gravity, but you can discern that it is there. From the coin that falls from your pocket to the moon that is held in its orbit, it's all about gravity. You can't see it, hear it, or smell it, yet it's there because it is an intangible force. You will only know of its existence the moment you observe relentlessly the effects that it casts on the things around it. Your eyes won't see that—only your mind will.

Just remember the illustration of gravity whenever you need to think about the invisible nature of all things whether that is the response of your friends to certain matters, the attraction of the girl walking into the room, or the effect of the master salesman on his client. Whatever is in front of you has its nature, and only your mind can observe and decipher it.

To observe with the mind, you have to first start with Contemplation Before the Fact. Once you do that, you will be able to have the framework that allows you to observe with the mind. Once you observe with the mind, then you will be able to expand your ability to Contemplate in real time, but that comes much later and after much practice as more and more associative factors come to the surface.

The Stoic observes all things with his mind. When he does, he realizes that he can alter the filter in which he observes things. He also slowly begins to realize that prejudice, bias, and negativity do not serve his purpose. It is one of the many reasons why you find that most Stoics are not biased in their opinion, and they make good judges and arbiters.

Bias and prejudice obscure the mind, and when the mind is the one that is used to observe things, it makes the person blind when there is prejudice in the equation. It becomes apparent to the Stoic that prejudice is counterproductive to his own efforts and to his own well-being. The infrequent times when prejudice may be of use become inconsequential to his efforts. He realizes that it is better for him, and it is for this selfish reason that he brings about the reasons to stave off prejudice and bias, and he looks to see things as they are and without any added flavor.

If you have ever played a musical instrument or a sport, such as tennis, you will know that practice makes perfect. When you start with a musical instrument, you need to look at the note, find the key, and then execute the note by pressing the key on the instrument. There is a path and a long chain of events that need to happen. The resulting sound that is produced by the instrument is staccato and never has the composer's intent, but it's the point to start from. As more practice is applied to the playing of the instrument, the transition from one note to the next eventually gets smoother, and the thread of the melody that emerges approximates the harmony the composer originally envisioned.

With more practice, not only does the resulting melody rise to the expectation of the composer, but it also lifts the hearts that listen to it because the player through countless hours of practice has tipped into the nature of the melody and the sound and delivered the resulting experience to the listener. The effect of his practice can be seen in the looks of pleasure in the audience that is within earshot of the player's recital.

What has all this to do with Real Time Contemplation? Real Time Contemplation is what you master with practice. The more you practice the art of contemplation, the more you will be able to do it seamlessly like the musician who played the piece of music seamlessly until the audience approves.

You should know that real time contemplation happens at a very deep level of the psyche and is never found at the conscious level of the mind. It is a subconscious process and one that you should know will happen in time but not something you can chase for in your endeavor to practice Stoicism.

It was mentioned before that you should not try to contemplate or reflect in the moment while you are experiencing an event. You can think about an event and make a decision on how to proceed, but you cannot analyze that event and contemplate it at the point of the event. How do we reconcile these two issues?

The first thing to recall is that real time contemplation happens in the subconscious of the mind just like the seasoned musician who plays his instrument after years of daily practice. He closes his eyes and cedes control of his hands and body to his subconscious mind that has every note, movement, and touch refined to the point of perfection. In the same way, once you have spent years practicing contemplation, the subconscious catches on and starts chewing the day's events in real time, and you allow it to do that without trying to rob it of its responsibility by giving it to the conscious mind. All you have to do after that is connect to the subconscious mind and look at the result it has processed.

The key then is to know how to keep your subconscious mind online and available in all situations when you need it. For the Stoic, after years of meditation and contemplation practice, his ability to turn to a subconscious process is almost automatic and instinctual. It is a side effect, one can say, of the perpetual silence that he practices. The more one engages in chatter, the more the disquiet mind suppresses the more powerful subconscious mind.

There are numerous ways to practice this. There is no easy way, but the one that is the most effective is to spend no less than two hours a day in contemplation and meditation and 95 percent of your time in silence throughout the day. If you do not need to talk, then don't. After silence becomes your way of life, your subconscious will be available to you more often, and you will see that you make better choices and decisions because the more powerful mind resides in the subconscious.

It is also important that you train the mind with periods of short meditative and mindful exercises during the course of the day. Set aside some time in the afternoon and one more time in the early evening for about ten minutes each to recharge the mind so that you can get in touch with the silence. It is a good way to also control the mind from getting too far into the challenges of the day at a conscious level. You have to learn to turn things off.

The power of Stoic Meditation and how to do it can be found in the next book in this series. Stoic meditation is very different from the other kinds of meditation that one could try. It is about getting in constant touch with the base of the mind so that you are able to process things accurately at a more rapid rate.

Chapter 9 - Nature and Stoicism

"All things are parts of one single system, which is called nature; the individual life is good when it is in harmony with nature."

— Zeno of Citium, Founder of Stoicism

There is a branch of science and design called biomimicry. It is the way designers observe nature to see how nature has evolved to solve various problems. Researchers and designers have found that there is a treasure trove of ideas found within the way nature solves its problems in the shared ecosystems.

In the same way, the Stoic is a natural at biomimicry. He is able to see the way nature responds to an issue and then adapts itself to embrace the issue and grow together or find a way to solve the problem in a way that is holistic and harmonious.

Take, for instance, the increase in population of jellyfish in certain oceans. Scientists were puzzled as to why some areas had a significantly higher population of these nasty stinging creatures and why in some other areas there were almost none. What they found was that these jellyfish thrive in polluted waters. They served a purpose of returning the polluted waters to a more balanced state. Once the water is returned to its unpolluted state, the jellyfish reduce in population or migrate away.

Jellyfish is nature's way of cleaning or returning the balance to its oceans. In the same way, the Stoic uses nature to interact with the environment around him. To be able to do this, he understands the nature of things, and then he is able to apply that nature to the outcome that he sees as best for the moment.

Two Classes of Nature

There are two kinds of nature in the Stoic's mind. The first is the kind of nature that you see around you, from the grass that grows underfoot to the clouds that appear overhead and everything that happens without the direct intervention of man's hand. These are the tangible aspects of nature. It is hard to describe this as the things that you can see because there are so many parts of this tangible nature that you can't see. Take, for instance, viruses and bacteria that can't be seen by the naked eye. They are still there, just too small to be seen. This is still a tangible phenomenon.

On the other hand, the example that we have seen in other parts of the book is the gravity that occurs between the earth and that which sticks to it or is in its orbit. No amount of magnifying power can see the gravity field that happens, and this is the intangible force of nature.

There you have one class of nature. It is the tangible and the intangible objects and forces that exist in the environment and universe around us.

Then comes the second class of nature. That is the nature of the way things happen or the course of things that are consequences of man. Man's pollution on the earth has become its own force of nature. Regardless of whether or not you believe in the problems of pollution, you cannot deny that it has an effect on the planet and the world around you. Mind you, it is not that pollution is a class of nature, but rather it is the conscious actions and sequence of consequences that become a force.

A lesser example would be the force that has resulted in a large swath of society to be obese and diabetic in the United States. This is also caused by the second class of nature. It is the forces of the masses that has resulted in poor eating habits and the rise in obesity. While one part of the planet languishes in hunger and starvation, the other languishes in obesity and eating disorders. Both are forces of this nature.

When one pulls back far enough, one is able to see the aggregate change in the state of affairs that is caused by the individual actions of all the inhabitants of a certain area. This becomes known as the nature of this area. This nature changes from place to place, and it is merely the aggregate action of individuals of the sample set and the consequences that they bring about intentionally or otherwise.

These are the two classes of nature that the Stoic is most concerned with.

The first is important but to a lesser degree than the second for understanding the actions of man. A Stoic does not seek to alter the actions or the choices of all men—only to understand them so that he can adapt his actions and understanding to better improve his long-term prospects and equity.

You will never find a Stoic in the midst of proselytizing or evangelizing his philosophy or beliefs. Even in the days of Socrates (who was not actually a Stoic) to the days of Plato and then to Agrippa and Chrissipus, none of them stood in the Agora and preached for the sake of gaining followers. They were there to discuss and refine their conclusions, and slowly men would listen and then join their discussion. It was never about head count and popularity.

To be a Stoic is to be able to understand the nature of all things. To understand the nature of all things, we know that we need to observe. We are not looking to learn nature the way the botanist would like to teach us. We are looking for the soul of nature that tells us how things behave in the midst of certain forces. Once we understand this, we are then able to navigate our way because you know that you need to learn about the way you perceive things, the way you react, and the way you are. Once you know the nature of your own existence and the nature of the world around you, then you can start to interact with it with better success and better outcomes.

For the purpose of this book, we will call it the Two-Class Nature model. This will help to see nature as not just the critters and the plants around us but the way all things in nature behave in static solitary conditions and in dynamic interactive conditions. It gives us the connection to the world beyond our own self and the nature that has influence over our life.

Iterative Contemplation

The Stoic practices constant and pensive thought because he is constantly paying attention to the world that is around him while his subconscious is iteratively making sense of all the data and is following through. It is far from reality to find a Stoic busy in chatter or prone to folly.

To be able to understand something, it is a dance that must happen between your mind, the conscious and the subconscious, and the reality that exists around you. This is the iterative process. It is like an engineer or a designer trying to mimic nature by building plane that can fly. He tries once and fails. He tries a second time and fails, and he goes on trying until he has worked out all the different issues that have not worked out down to the last detail. Then, low and behold, the idea works. He successfully gets his creation to mimic nature. In this case, he builds a contraption that flies and mimics birds.

Mistakes are just the trigger that starts the iterative process in the execution of an idea. How then does iteration work in contemplation? Well, in pretty much the same way. When a Stoic Contemplates Before the Fact or his subconscious contemplates in real time, he is constantly going back and forth between the outcome he is trying to get to and the outcome that is happening to find where he is making the mistake or where he is doing the right thing.

Iterative contemplation cannot be done by the conscious mind alone. It would drive any human being crazy. Iterative contemplation happens in the subconscious with some help from the conscious. It is like an endless loop in a computer algorithm that keeps analyzing the occurrence in nature and then throwing "what-if" scenarios to see if the outcome starts to approximate the desired result.

Iterative Contemplation works very well in the Two-Class Nature model. Once you are able to constantly iterate between what happens in nature and what happens within you, it is easier to be more predictive of what happens for each action that you initiate.

It is hardly ever the case that Stoics, who are experienced in life, make mistakes when they place themselves on the short end of the stick. Remember that the Stoic only sees the consequence of his actions in the context of the nature that surrounds and permeates him. In this regard, the next section about good and bad, right and wrong comes into play.

Good and Bad

There are only two forms of nature in this universe as far as the Stoic is concerned. There is no good or bad, saint or sinner, angel or demon. The Stoic sees all things as they are and not with the binary bifocals that most people tend to judge events. He does not see something as good just because it agrees with his sensibilities, and he does not see something as bad just because it doesn't.

Good and bad are mere labels that the man who cannot think, contemplate, or reflect has on events that are in front of him. He who lives on dogma, rules, and commandments is only protected from basic folly. He will never be able to be more than that or contribute more than that. A man who understands the root of that dogma and sees things as not merely good and bad but rather on a scale of actions, consequences, and events beyond one's control is then able to move past the labels that limit him from being more than just a vassal for other people's experiences.

To make it simple, there is no good or bad. All things are just what they are. Good or bad is a judgment that one makes to be able to classify a set of actions that they feel they should not do. Let's say you put speeding in the bad column instead of the good column. If you do that and one day as you are driving and your friend in the passenger seat experiences a burst appendix and you have to rush him to the hospital, would you still be thinking that speeding is bad? If something is bad, should it not be always bad? Why would it be acceptable one day and not the next?

The same can be seen for issues of good. What if you have an accident and you are given morphine for the pain while the broken leg heals. Is morphine good or bad? Well, in this case it is good, but what if you took it when there wasn't a medical reason to do so? Is it bad then?

A Stoic does not judge things to be good or bad but views them holistically based on the situation and the consequence of the issue. He chooses not to label the morphine as bad or the speeding as good but rather understands the nature of both and uses them when it is appropriate. Once again taking into consideration the long-term consequences of the action. He still does not classify things as good or bad.

In the case of the morphine, if the doctor prescribes the medication for him and he asks the doctor about the chances of addiction in taking the morphine and the doctor says that it is fairly certain that he will go through a severe withdrawal process, the Stoic would most likely choose the pain of the broken limb now rather than the pain of withdrawal later.

The Stoic one must remember is always balancing the present gain to the long-term consequences of his actions.

Advanced Stoic Concepts in Nature

Above all else, you have to find truth in nature. When your life and truth are in harmony with that nature, then you will find that all things flow smoothly, and you are able to achieve more since you are carried by the wind and tide of nature rather than hindered by it.

Stoics observe all things and contemplate the observation so that they can understand nature. If you have made it this far in this book, that much should be clear by now. You cannot go against nature, and if you do, be prepared that the hull of your vessel will buckle under the pressure when you least expect it. The catastrophic consequence is certainly.

Rethink your perspective and appreciation of nature. It is not just the trees and the critters that are a part of nature. It is also the movement of all things and the behavior of all things. Nature extends from beyond the void of space all the way to the point before the Big Bang. The universe includes light and darkness, matter and energy as well as forces of gravity, attraction, repulsion, and all those things that you learned about in science class.

But it is still more than that. The Stoic does not need to know how the nebulous gases in space works. He just needs to know that they're there. More importantly, he needs to understand how all things move and react. He needs to understand the nature of the human spirit and the nature of the human mind, and even more, the nature of the combined mind and spirit.

The scope of nature is broad, and you do not need to try to understand all of it in one fell swoop. Instead, you need to start to understand it step-by-step.

Just as the Stoic reflects on his actions to better understand his own nature, the Stoic also contemplates objects that are the focus of study to understand their nature. Between meditation, concentration, reflection, and now contemplation, it may seem that they are many words to describe what is essentially an introspective dynamic. That is true to a certain extent, but the Stoic seeks out and sharpens numerous tools to find the truth.

The distinction between these introspective tools may be lost on many who do not yet practice. In time, the mind will get out of its own way, and the spirit will rise to resonate with all things around it, and then we will become one with what we observe. This then leads us to believe that we are gravitating toward metaphysics, and to most metaphysicists this is a little too far in the fringe.

But for now let us not push the envelope that it touches the boundaries of the metaphysical world, although it is not hard to believe whatever is in the next layer has to come into contact with the current layer simply because that is the way one element comes into contact with the next.

Think of it as the layers of the Grand Canyon— the strata of fossilized rock frozen in time into a visual record of history. Each layer does not live in distinction of the previous or the next layer. There is a boundary layer that exists between them where the two layers form a third. It's like the brackish water that exists between the freshwater of the river and the saltwater of the ocean. In the same way, the metaphysical layer is the boundary layer between the tangible world and the intangible world. That boundary layer is what we touch when we dive into the world of metaphysics.

The mind is such that it forms a boundary layer as well. It exists between the subject and the object. In philosophy and in Stoicism especially, the philosophers are constantly thinking about the nature of things, and the relationship between subject and object stands center stage. The subject is us, our physical presence. It includes the form of all things that make up what we are. It even plays host to all the things that make up who we are.

Thus, it is the mind that stands between the two helping to decipher and process the object so that the subject can become one with the tangible and intangible phenomena that exists around all of us and, in fact, is a part of us.

Metaphysics is baked into Stoicism. It was originally the work of Plato to a certain degree and then went on to become the life's work of Aristotle. Plato and Aristotle, who were both heavily influenced by Socrates, went on to develop different schools of thought and injected their perspective into the development of different lines of philosophy, which were then amalgamated in the mind of Zeno of Citium.

Metaphysics is not the core of Stoicism, but it inadvertently becomes a part of the layer between subject and object. Metaphysics comes under the branch of Stoic Physics, which is the movement of the body (any body in space, not just the human body). In Stoic Physics, the actors on the stage of the universe are divided into two areas: matter and pneuma. We have seen this earlier but using different terms. We alluded to it in terms of tangible and intangible, or physical objects and their nature. In Stoic terms, they were labeled as matter and pneuma. Matter being all things that were tangible all the way down to atoms and subatomic particles, and pneuma that described the non-particle phenomena.

The interaction of them and the realm of the pneuma was of particular interest to metaphysicists. You can see it in the language development of the Stoics. After Aristotle, the matter in the matter-pneuma relationship was renamed to take on a deeper extent of the phenomenon. It was called substrate, and so the relationship became the substrate-pneuma duality.

This is where the duality of man comes from in modern philosophy. It sits at the heart of substrate pneuma, where there are two states colocated with the being. In some philosophies, this is unacceptable, and in Stoicism it is baked in. So the philosophies debate this endlessly. In the end, it is semantics because matter itself is the co-location of two states—substrate and pneuma.

Think about this in modern physics. Objects we see every day are made up of molecules, which are made of atoms. Atoms are made of protons, neutrons, and electrons. Those are, in turn, made from something called quarks. Quarks are then made up of vibration energy as described in string theory. In essence, the Stoics were right according to modern physics. Matter is made up of energy at its most fundamental level, and it is the same energy that gives rise to forces. This duality of matter and energy is real and provable.

Putting the physics behind us, then it is time to ponder the meaning of all this. Concentration in Stoics opens up the mind to the metaphysical boundary of all things and allows the mind to get greater insight into the nature of things. Our mind, after all, is made up of both substrate and pneuma. It is made of neurons and synaptic bridges that hold character of both these phenomena.

The brain and the mind that is built on top of it are merely the bridge between the subject and the object or at least has the ability to be. Just like a hard drive that you pick up at the tech store, it is useless when first unboxed. It only contains the matter (parts and casing). Until you actually put information in, nothing can be said of the drive. It is not worth more than the materials it took to make it or the cost to replace it. But once you fill it with information, the value of the drive becomes something altogether different.

When the brain takes on information, it physically changes and becomes a lot more powerful and a lot more valuable that increases the bridge between the subject and the object until such a time the Stoic becomes highly intuitive that the ability to predict future events extends further down the horizon.

Think about that for a minute. It almost seems that the Stoic is a mythical being with powers beyond what ordinary humans have. If you think about it, you will realize that if a computer could be built that could crunch enough data points, it would be able to predict exactly when it would rain. If one could observe all the factors of the weather, predicting what happens next is not such a far leap. We do it with fairly good accuracy right now. We can predict general weather up to a week from now. We can predict it with better accuracy three days out, and we can predict with higher probability tomorrow's weather. That predictive ability comes from observing the cause and effect that leads to rain. That's what a Stoic does. He observes the cause and the effect—the nature and the substrate and, in time, he knows what is going to happen next. The older and more experienced the Stoic gets, the more accurate his predictions.

Ultimately, it comes back to contemplation. One can choose to look at contemplation as what one would like to have for lunch today, or one could contemplate much larger issues in the world.

How large an issue one gets to contemplate is a function of how much observation and reflection (study) one does, and how deep one's meditation (silence) is what determines how far the Stoic goes.

Chapter 10 - Pleasure and Contentment

The Stoic sees pleasure in a way that most of us do not. Stoics are meager in their existence to the point that they can sometimes be mistaken as Ascetics, but they are not. Stoics choose simplicity in living because they understand the nature of the human condition and the nature of the senses as one that dulls with time, and that dulling of the senses requires that additional doses of the pleasure needs to be brought to bear to be able to have the same pleasure.

It is the same with addicts. The addict of a substance today may take that substance in small quantities and then as the effect of that substance wears off takes more to return to that state of pleasure. In time, more and more is needed to have the same effect. This is the reason addicts become the way they do. We are all addicts of one thing or another. For some of us, it is work; for some, it's food; or for some of us, it is tobacco or alcohol. We all have substances that we take in increasing quantities to have the same effect.

The Stoic understands the nature of pleasure and the nature of contentment. He doesn't categorize the consequence of addiction as something that is bad or the state of not being addicted as good. He just sees one as more beneficial in the long run than the other.

For this reason, pleasure is not a consideration of the Stoic. For most people, the moment they know that pleasure is not the goal of the Stoic, it becomes the deal breaker. In fact, the Stoic actually goes a little out of his way to tune his body to not seek out pleasure. By doing this, he is able to avoid certain actions that may diminish his ability to evaluate or understand the nature that surrounds him.

Ego

The element that helps to elevate pleasure and contentment in the mind of a person is the element of ego. The ego is the intangible figment of the mind that mimics what it thinks this body and this mind that resides within it is. The ego, when it has an accurate depiction of the real, results in good consequences. The ego that thinks itself worse off than it really is has a detrimental consequence just as the ego that thinks itself to be more than it really is. The Stoic is not one to boost the power of the ego or to increase its existence in any form.

In modern psychology terms, there are various forms of ego. There is the inner self, in terms of the Id and the Super Ego, but these are not the issues with the Stoic. After all, Sigmund Freud and Carl Jung were all psychologists who came a millennia after the philosophers of Stoicism.

Stoics see ego as the thing in us that looks for the superficial benefit in the here and now rather than the real benefit over the course of the long term. The ego is anathema to the Stoic. Because of this outlook, the Stoic is careful to not engage in any activity that has the effect of expanding the ego or to promote it in any way.

There are a number of ego-promoting tools that the Stoic avoids. The first is the manner in which he dresses. The Stoic chooses to live a simple life so that he is not bombarded with the effects of the ego. One such person was Augustus Caesar. This is not to say that Augustus was Stoic, but he lived his life in such a way that it adhered to the values of the Stoics in ancient Greece. He wore simple clothes and even slept in a chamber that had a simple hay bed and ate simple food, e.g., yogurt, nuts, cheese, and fruit. He was unlike any of the other emperors that came after him who would live large and extravagant lifestyles.

His primary reason was that he didn't want it to cloud his mind. Stoics are the same way. They do not want the lifestyle to expand the ego, which then could cloud their judgment in what they do. Once the ego comes into existence and finds pleasure in the things that inflate it, the ego starts to grow to the point that it wants to only spend the time it has to feed itself. Even food becomes a question of ego, not a question of sustenance. A person who has inflated his ego would choose food for the purpose of feeding his ego and not feeding his body.

When one eats to feed the ego, they feel pleasure. When one eats to satisfy his nutritional needs, he is content. The Stoic looks for contentment and not pleasure in all he does. Pleasure is a physical feeling that we have within us. It was placed there during the forces of evolution so as to be able to survive. It was there before the mind came into existence, and it works as a form of punishment and reward to get the body to do certain things it needs to do.

But that purpose of the pleasure centers has been altered by the forces around us. We, as a society, have become so caught up with the pleasure centers that we have forgotten that contentment leads to happiness, but pleasure has its consequences down the road.

How often do we make mistakes that were goaded on by the pleasure-seeking centers in our body and mind? But when we seek contentment, the same consequences give us a long-term benefit.

Contentment

Contentment is not the same as pleasure. Pleasure is ephemeral and inconsistent. It extracts a cost to experience it. Contentment, which is often mistaken for pleasure, is the opposite. It does not extract anything in the future. It is what you work for, and it is equitable. When you put in a hard day's work, you find that the rewards make you feel content. When you steal something, there is the sudden burst of pleasure in getting something for nothing, but there is no long-term contentment. In the end, the pleasure of the forbidden fruit passes, and the time to pay the piper arrives. It will extract more than the value of what has been spent, but the rewards for honest work will not be spent unnecessarily.

This is the benefit of contentment and just an illustration. The Stoic is interested in contentment, not in pleasure. Even if he does engage in activities that may bring pleasure, he is not addicted to that pleasure and does the activity for the sake of the activity. The difference being the way Augustus Cesar ate food, which brings contentment, to the way Emperor Nero gorged himself with lavish meals for pleasure.

There is another aspect to pleasure that needs to be understood that is part of the Stoic's innate nature. Pleasure is a physical attribute. Contentment is a mental and spiritual attribute. The preference of contentment over pleasure signifies the growth of a man from beast to intellectual.

All of mankind evolved from lower levels of creatures. That evolution left the mind wired in ways that are needed to facilitate life and growth. But at this point, as human beings, man has the opportunity to reach a higher level, and that higher level is the level of contentment versus the level of pleasure. Stoicism is not about visceral and physical payoffs but rather spiritual and cerebral contentment. To be able to experience contentment, the Stoic is able to elevate himself in thought and deed. It also acts as a guardrail. If the Stoic feels that he is gravitating toward pleasure, then he knows that his entire mental state is in decline and that he is reverting to his former physical and base self.

The Stoic's ability to live a clean life is not from discipline but from purpose. It is like the child and his parent. The parent tells the child not to eat candy because the parent understands the detrimental effects to the point that he has no interest in it. He places this as a rule for his child who doesn't know better. The child obeys the rule but secretly desires the candy. On some days, he needs to be able to have significant discipline to be able to overcome his urge. On other days, he breaks down and has a piece of candy and then feels guilty about it. He is forgiven, and then he starts again.

In the case of the Stoic, he is like the father who understands the reason behind not doing something or the reason for doing something is that he is not overcome by the bodily urges to be attracted to that which would give him pain as a consequence down the road.

The path from pleasure to contentment is not a direct path, and it is not the reason one begins the journey. No one starts an arduous journey by saying they want to stop feeling pleasure to be able to start feeling contentment. Instead, the journey is about living a normal existence and then elevating one's existence to being one that is higher. At that point, one feels contentment and places more importance on it than any kind of pleasure that could be offered to him.

Chapter 11 - A Stoic's Path

Much of what has already been discussed up to this point is the path that a novice takes on his way to becoming a Stoic. As has already been stated, the novice is not conferred the membership or bestowed the honor. A Stoic is as a Stoic does. A person is Stoic if he behaves in a manner that is considered to be Stoic. He does not need to even read one verb of any manuscript from any Greek or Latin text to be able to say that he is or isn't Stoic. If he were to incorporate the virtues that he masters of Stoicism and the philosophers of the Agora had debated and thought so hard about, then he is all the better for it because he has found the truth of Stoicism within himself. He may then choose to call himself a Stoic or be referred to by any other name. That is not important, but a person who understands the nature for the Stoic would see the person and know that this person is authentic.

There are many of those people in the world, who go by many names and hail from many lands. They are masters of various industries and disciplines, yet they all embody the spirit of the Stoic Master. Stoicism is not the exclusive property of Western civilization. There are many in the Far East and Middle East who embody the spirit of the Stoic. There are many in the Far West that are the same too. The point is not about the name. The point is about the action.

Some of the men who have been Stoic in nature are the likes of Mohandas Gandhi, the man who liberated India from British colonialism without firing a single shot. He did it with purely Stoic manners and Stoic strategies. Never once did he tell a lie in his negotiations and never once did he show anything but strength in his efforts. He was repeatedly jailed, yet he persisted because he had determined that the truth of the matter was that home rule was better than the whip of a foreign power.

Albert Einstein, just like Gandhi, was a dyed-in-the wool Stoic. His search for the truth in all things is what led him to the scientific discoveries that he made and the Nobel Prize that he won.

In the same token, Thomas Jefferson was also one who was an honorary Stoic. He never claimed to be one, but it is very likely, based on his demeanor and his actions, that he was Stoic in nature, thought, and deed. When the British were chasing him after the Assembly in Virginia had fled the capital, he had gone to Monticello, his home in the western edges of Virginia. When he was brought the news that the British troops were on their way there, he packed up his family, placed them in a carriage, and gently went back to his study to save the papers of state secrets and of national importance. All of this without once running or tripping over himself. Never once did he raise his voice to his servants in a tone of hurried excitement. He just went rapidly but gracefully from one task to the next before mounting his horse and slipping out through the woods mere seconds before the British troops arrived. That was just his demeanor, but his actions and thoughts were no different. He had been born into wealth, and he had slaves in employment by his family since the day he was born. It should have been commonplace for him to think that slaves were a regular element of the era and nothing to think about.

But he showed great Stoic virtue when he gradually started to think of the equity of all of it and the unfairness to treat a man and rob him of his freedom when the truth about all of this shows that we are free regardless of color or creed. That must have been his greatest indicator to the world that he was Stoic by nature. In fact, some of his favorite writings were by Cato, who himself was a Stoic stalwart in the days of the Roman Empire.

There are three kinds of Stoics. It doesn't matter which one you are. You are either born a Stoic, meaning that you feel it in your heart that the truth is the most important virtue in all of life. Nothing else matters. The truth that you seek supersedes all notions, dogmas, and ideals. It stands the test of time, and you can feel it in your soul. From that constantly visceral and resonating feeling, you start your journey to become the bearer and the beacon of truth. If this is you, then you do not need books and manuscripts to tell you that you are Stoic. You just are.

Then there are those who don't know it, but once they learn about it, they can't do anything else but follow it. They understand the concept of it, and it then starts to resonate within them. They see it in all they do, and they gain momentum on a daily basis as they work toward the ultimate peace that the Stoic enjoys by knowing that his path is right and true.

Finally, there are those who hear the term "Stoic" and want to be it. They want to adorn the crown or wear the badge that reads S-T-O-I-C, and they want to tell the world that they are part of the philosophy of the Emperor Marcus Aurelius. But they do not understand the importance of truth, and they are quick to believe lies and even quicker to tell them. These are not Stoics, and many fall into this category. They know how to memorize books and manuscripts that have been translated from the ancients, yet they do not know how to adapt it to today's world. These are not Stoics. But there is hope. They still need to incorporate the ideas and live the words.

A Stoic's path is easy if one is not too immersed in the world of today. There is a significant problem that most Stoic teachers do not talk about, and that is that the time in which Stoicism is facing its revival is exactly the time that it is hardest to survive and thrive. It is a paradox to be contemplated, but it is nonetheless true.

The paradox we are faced with is that the time we are facing in the world is fundamentally flawed because we are bombarded with such advanced technology and such runaway commercialism that the typical person is not ready for the degree of assault that is targeted at the senses and sensibilities.

Take the issue of minimalism. There is a movement toward minimalism today, but it is in the context of materialism that minimalism is looked at. Ironic but prevalent. In the same way, Stoics are not about riches, although they end up being wealthy, but most novices today are looking for a means to train their mind so that they can become wealthy. In essence, they are searching for a means to materialism and wealth by using a power that is bestowed on those who are not seeking materialism and wealth. As I said, ironic.

The problem lies in the fact that happiness is seen through the eyes of the modern world, and that happiness is taken to sprout from things. And what better way to have more things than to have more money? The more money you have, the more things you can get. So the cycle is perpetuated.

What does the path of the Stoic finally entail? What is in it for all the effort that it takes to be on this path? The answer is that it endows peace on the person who understands the truth. This life is not about going to work on a daily basis and collecting a paycheck in a fortnight. This world is not about the latest vehicle or the latest fashion. There is so much more that the human mind and body are capable of, yet we are stuck with just appreciating and looking forward to measly things that bring about fleeting happiness.

Stoics seek truth because they know that truth bestows perpetual happiness to the mind, body, and soul. It is not a fleeting pleasure in the body. It is lasting. There is a reason behind this life, and the path to the truth reveals the purpose that each of us is essentially looking for. It is the materialism that distracts us and makes us think that that new model BMW is the answer to what we are craving for on the inside. But after getting that new and shiny, curvy sedan, we find a month later that that's not it, so we slump back down and look for something else. Sound familiar?

Minimalism?

That is materialism. It is designed to be fleeting so that you can go out and buy something else, but that is what needs to stop. You cannot hope to embrace Stoicism if you are busy waiting to buy the latest thing or fill your home with things you do not really need.

Part of the path that you would need to take is to start thinking about what you own. It is not a bad thing to own things, but it is a distraction to want to buy more and to clutter yourself with more. Earlier in the book, we briefly mentioned Augustus Caesar and the quarters he slept in. It was a simple dwelling for one of the world's richest men of the time, but he did that to keep his heart and mind pure and uncluttered.

A Stoic is someone who sees this plainly. He does not see it as minimalism or decluttering. There are no fancy names to it. He just does not desire more things. You need to find a way that you can reduce most of what you have in your life.

Whether that means you have to sell some of your possessions or put them in a storage unit is up to you. There are no hard-and-fast rules. If you undertake the path to Stoicism, then you will get the idea that you need to worry less about this and focus more on the truth.

The same applies for the way one dresses and the way one approaches fashion. This is not to say that you have to resort to walking around like Diogenes. Instead, you have to look at what is necessary. If you need to wear a suit to the office, by all means, but it does not have to be a suit that is exorbitantly expensive. A suit that wears neatly and is tidy will more than suffice, and you should be strong enough to be able to rely on your own abilities and knowledge than to rely on the expensive clothes you are wearing. Shakespeare says that you should "costly thy habit as thy purse can buy." He is trying to tell his audience that it is acceptable to dress up to the level you can afford but not more than that. It is pretty certain among Stoic circles that Shakespeare was a Stoic. Whether or not he knew it is unclear, but he certainly fits the bill.

There is a path that takes you from where you are to the point of being a Stoic. That path is not something that is the same for everyone. The only thing that is the same is the destination. It's like we are all over the country, but we are looking to get to Wichita, Kansas. The destination is all the same for us, but the path for someone who comes from Albany is going to be very different from the path that the lady from Los Angeles is going to take. The key is to understand the destination and then find the path to get there using truth as your guide.

Creator

Stoics are firm believers in evolution. If nothing else, it is a good place to start to understand the meaning of all things. Look at the creation of the Grand Canyon. It is a sort of evolution. First, you find that layer upon layer is built to create this stratified mass of earth. Then the coursing of the Colorado River over millions of years cuts a path through this stratified layer. The evidence is there, and the evidence is logical and reasonable. It is something that the Stoics believe can happen instead of the canyon just being there.

They realize that nature had to build it, and nature had to carve it. It didn't happen overnight. Do the Stoics believe in God because they believe in evolution? Yes, of course. The Stoics believe in God but in a very clear and provable way. Do they evangelize the existence of God? No. The reason they do not evangelize the existence of God or the benefits of being Stoic is because each person's path courses a different vein, and it must be traveled alone and without coercion.

The topic of evolution is offered as an illustration. It is to show that the Stoic finds common ground and balance between technology and science. A Stoic is free to believe in the gods of his childhood and youth. When he is ready, he begins to question his religion, but more often than not, he does not become agnostic or atheistic but rather finds a deeper meaning in the words that are presented in the text of his scripture.

Evidence of the existence of the power greater than all of the universe or one that unites us is readily available to all those who ponder. The Stoic is constantly on a quest to seek this truth and to understand the existence of man, nature, and the Providence of a higher existence. We tend to call this God in the theological sense, but the true Stoic seeks to unshackle himself from the mundane and often repeated explanations that border on tales.

The Stoic sits on the fence not because he is indecisive but because he is weighing all the possible evidence and parsing the language that is being repeated. Many of those who evangelize rarely understand the text they are using as the basis for their efforts to convince, and the Stoic understands this. But he is looking for the truth, and in so doing he gives the presenter a chance to explain himself.

The Stoic is on a quest to find God and the mysteries that surround the universe to a greater degree than the man who is blindly evangelizing. The difference is that the Stoic is willing to listen to reason and evidence. He is also fully aware that the greatest evidence of a supreme being is right in front of all of us, but he is still in search for what that means.

It is incorrect to assume that Stoics are atheists or agnostic. They are not either by default, but they are in search. They do have the power of faith, but they do not misplace that faith. They are also respective of religion and the various perspectives that the different religions offer.

Stoics, even if they cannot find the necessary evidence of a divine being in the way that they would like, still turn to prayer on a regular basis. The inconsistency is perplexing to the novice who does not understand how one can be uncertain of the mode to pray in and the direction to aim that prayer but still be sure that the prayer is necessary.

The reason for this is that prayer is a powerful tool that works regardless of the deity it is directed at. Being human, the Stoic understands that we need something for the senses to consume so that it can trigger the spirit. That something to focus on is the tangible statue or act that is required. The Stoic is certain that God, or whatever power that is responsible for everything, is not in solid form and looks like something that is familiar to a person on this planet. The Stoic is certain that the creation of objects is to focus the mind so that the soul can reach out and touch the divine.

The reason for raising the issue of creation is to achieve dual purpose. The first is to illustrate the thinking of the Stoic. The second is to highlight the issue in itself and dispel the notion that Stoics are anti-creator or anti-God. They are neither. They have strong faith, strong beliefs, and deeply believe in the power of prayer.

Chapter 12 - Stoicism and the Modern World

It is hard to reconcile Stoic values and the modern world as we have alluded to in the rest of this book. The verbiage and the philosophies as well as the anecdotes and references are ancient in their origin. That mismatch has an unintended effect on those who are trying to make Stoicism work in the modern age. But it can be done.

As you have seen in the rest of the book, there are a number of practices that the Stoic uses that fit naturally into the modern world, and we have not really used the ancient references to relate them. But they are nonetheless based on ideas that are more than two thousand years old. It's just that we didn't put them in that context.

It's great to read the books that were written by Emperor Marcus Aurelius or the slave Epictetus or Seneca for that matter, but the point that one must keep in mind about the references that they make have no basis in the modern world today. You could not live in a barrel and spend your days naked at your local grocer as Diogenes did in Athens. You could not live off the kindness of passersby and take the food that they may give you in exchange for words of wisdom that you find while you spend your life under the bridge.

The actions of Diogenes, Zeno, and Crastes are all not possible to be replicated in today's world. Does that mean we are not going to be able practice Stoicism? On the contrary, not only are we able to practice it, but we are also able to emulate much of what the ancients talked about but with a few twists.

The thing to consider is that the modern world differs from the ancient world in two main areas. The first is the technology that drives us, and the second is the socially acceptable areas that define us. Other than that, we are really pretty much the same species doing the same things that the people did in Athens a long time ago. Parents still fuss over their children, and children still disobey their parents. Friends still get together and talk about the latest events, and husbands and wives still have kitchen table issues just as they did back then.

Could the difference in technology mean that we get our information and pass it on differently from the way it was done back then? Well, not really. We still read books, but this time we can get them from Amazon. We can still hear teachers preach philosophy and accept that the marketplace is not called the Agora. It's called YouTube, and there are hundreds of various philosophers trying to hawk their brand of philosophy just as there were back at the Agora. Not everyone who preached or taught became a famed philosopher.

So what stayed the same?

The novice stayed the same. The novice had the power of resonance. Whatever he read, regardless of the words used, would resonate in the heart of the man who heard what he needed to hear. When Zeno heard Crastes speak, he was instantly perked up and became alert, and the message resonated with him. It doesn't matter if they rode horses and we fly in planes or future generations zip around in spaceships. What matters is that the person listening still has the same ability to pick up what he needs when he needs it so that he can proceed on his way the development of the philosophy that best resonates with him. That is another reason that no one should proselytize.

A second point is that social issues define us. Social issues account for a large part of who we are. Portals such as Facebook and Twitter bring large groups of people together and place an even higher burden of compliance on our shoulders. If it is not popular, we loathe to do it. If we like something and it does not get a thumbs-up or retweeted, we become an anxious wreck. That sense of social homogeneity is a major force in our life. That is a serious factor in the quest toward being a Stoic. A Stoic's path is solitary. You may need to have friends around you to bounce ideas off of or echo an idea, but that is not the best way to go about it. This is not like a chess club or a fraternity.

Stoicism is not about group-think. It is about the time you spend alone in the presence of the universe and the silence that allows your mind to rise above the surface. This has changed since the days of the Agora. Back then Stoicism was in its youth and still being debated and analyzed. It was not just the idea of one man. It was the amalgamation of various schools of thought collated by one man and then fiercely debated by supporters and detractors. Then that went through decades of further analysis and then was shipped to Rome, where it was taken up and analyzed again.

Today, it is being pieced back together in an attempt to apply it to today's problems and issues. It doesn't matter what today's issues really are because the practice of Stoic values and the tenets of Stoic philosophy are timeless in effect and effective in strategy.

Perhaps the main question that every novice getting started should pose is "Why Stoicism?" What about Stoicism makes it interesting? It is not a trick question. It actually is designed to bring the motives to the surface because if there is one thing that Stoics believe it's that there are messages in all intuitive acts, and they should be analyzed, not blindly followed.

In modern-day metaphysics and spirituality, there are many Stoic values and concepts that have guided themselves in different ways. We have seen one earlier in the book about minimalism, but there are more. The Law of Attraction is also a Stoic offshoot but with more contemporary vernacular used in its description.

Resonating with Information

We learned a great many things when we were children, and as children we naturally formed certain prejudices and biases about something we learned, as our senses were not fully developed for understanding the matter at hand. It is thus necessary that at some point in our life to look back on all the things we learned as children and doubt it. We must review and analyze it to find the truth in what we thought was undoubtedly true.

We should make it so that we see all we are doubting as false—in the beginning. This allows us to go about our business in a much better fashion without confusion or chaos and by easier means come to the truth and what is most certain.

This doubt that we apply to our knowledge should be applied to only that. It cannot be used in other aspects of our life for it will stop us from living. If we doubt everything in our life and in real time, then when it comes time for us to act or move, we will simply stand there unsure of what to do.

Unintentionally, our doubt extends to things that are indeed of sense. This is so because we are aware that our senses have betrayed us from time to time, and thus we cannot be certain about what is true and what is false. And we know that we should doubt everything we know because we understand that once tricked you can't give unending trust again to your not entirely reliable senses. This doubt is akin to the kind mentioned earlier where one doubts everything, and this is so because when we are always unsure of what's around us due to our knowing that our senses are sometimes unreliable. This doubt is perhaps the most dangerous, as it does not allow us to tell between our dreams and easily. For in dreams, we see things that are both real and conjured by the experiments of our mind. This coupled with our doubt of everything puts us in a state in which we cannot tell reality from dream.

We also doubt things that for the better part are proven true. Such things are included in the realm of mathematics, which are most conceptualized. This happens because we are doubting whether or not God, whom we know is an all-powerful entity that created us, made us such that things are untruthful for us from time to time. And we think this because we happen upon these instances quite often, and as we think that an all-powerful force is what created us, we think we are cursed with disloyal senses.

Chapter 13 - Divinity and Stoicism

In turns out that there is a lot of Stoic philosophy contained within Christian teachings. Just as metaphysics was baked into Stoic values and teachings, Stoic values and teachings are baked into the philosophy of Roman Catholic tenets.

When Emperor Constantine had decided to officially recognize the Catholic religion it was in part because there was already a movement in the provinces of Rome. He also realized that the Roman Empire was weakening, and that one good way to continue the empire was through the Catholic religion. During the Council of Nicaea, he presided over the compilation of the New Testament and the Bible so that Catholics could unite under a common teaching—one that was sanctioned by the once emperor, now pope.

By the time Constantine had come into power, Stoicism had been in the vein of the ruling class and the philosophers that occupied the capital.

The Catholic religion was then infused by the philosophy of Constantine, and the Bible was inadvertently shaped in that form.

Just as Socratic methods and Platonic ideals made their way into Stoicism, so too did Stoicism make its way into Catholicism and all the other Christian churches that sprung henceforth.

But the question now is to what extent does divinity play in the ideals of a Stoic? It is really the reverse of the question. What influence does Stoicism have on modern religions? We have seen the direct influence from ancient Stoicism to early Christianity, but what about what divinity occupies the annals of Stoic philosophy? It is easy to see that religion was not a part of Socratic thinking, but it did make its way into Stoic thinking because of the other influence that came as a part of it.

When we look at the nature of Stoicism, we start to see that it seeks the truth, and in so doing it approaches the universe with a mind that sees the whole and not just the parts. While Stoics do not see God the way it is depicted in the Sistine

Chapel, they understand that the nature of all things are parts of the divine.

Forget for a minute that religion exists. Put aside any thought or notion that the teachings and creation of man have anything to do with divinity. But then if you look at the universe and all that is in it, you will find that human existence in the universe has no bearing on it. Nature existed before us, and nature will continue to exist after us. In philosophy, that is called the necessary condition. Nature—pneuma and substrate—is the necessary condition for all other things. Without that the universe will not exist and neither will man. Without nature (once again, we are not talking birds, critters, and plants), humans will not exist. We are the contingent aspect of the equation, while nature is the necessary aspect of it.

Nature doesn't need us, but we need nature. We are derived from nature. Our body is 80 percent water by weight that means hydrogen and oxygen. The rest of our body is composed of carbon, nitrogen, calcium, and phosphorus. In other words, 99 percent of us is made up of these five elements. The other 1 percent is made of a few more elements (not more than six or seven), and that's how we exist.

Those dozen elements are part of nature. Without humans, those elements will exist; without those elements, we will not exist. We are not necessary for nature to exist, yet we are here. Whatever conclusion you can draw from that will take the powers of meditation, reflection, and contemplation to understand, and that shall be your homework.

The point is that Stoics believe that we are the manifestation of all the pneuma and substrate to result in a full body. You can think of the pneuma as the soul, and that all the combined pneuma and substrate in the universe is part of the energy field. That is the ultimate fabric of nature, and that is the divine that Stoics think of.

As you can tell, the Stoic is not interested in simple binary answers, and so personifications of powers and nature into human form is not something that they are interested in, but they understand that it is what many need to be able to invoke the faith that is needed to be able to elevate their spirits to a higher realm.

Chapter 14 - Forgiveness and Peace

If you have the power to see all things, one of the first things that you will come to realize is that there are flaws in all things that we see, especially in the level of accuracy and intention. It is not difficult to fall into a state of being perpetually cynical of the world. The Stoic is not a cynical person. He is just honest about the state of things.

The question then is whether the Stoic is forgiving or blind to the inconsistencies of man and word. The answer is complex, but that arc of the answer bends toward understanding and forgiveness when enough time has passed.

Without forgiveness, the Stoic's life would become dark. Because he sees all things after some time has passed, all he will see is the people around him being selfish and conceited no matter what they say. This would make for a miserable life. He then comes to the fork in the road, and he has to choose whether to overlook or correct the faults of others.

This is where it becomes a matter of survival paralleling a matter of intellectual pursuit. Forgiveness, it turns out, is not about the transgressor. It's about the transgressed. If the Stoic is the kind of person that understands the truth of all things, then he should also learn the overarching truth of the fact that most human beings are in various states of learning. Imagine if you are subjected to first graders all the time and you think that the world consists of only first-graders (an absurd thought to be sure, but it's a thought experiment). Then what would you think of the world's ability to do long division? Would you not think then that everyone in the world has no ability to do long division? Let's say that the world is indeed filled with first graders. Then wouldn't it be acceptable that they do not know how to perform long division? It is fully reasonable. That is the first face of forgiveness. It isn't the forgiveness that one expects. Forgiveness is usually thought of as the ability to pardon a mistake.

Now let's look at how it feels, even if feeling is not one of the tools of the Stoic. If he does not see the point that the first grader does not have the prerequisite skill to do long division, then it is entirely possible that it would be frustrating. But the truth of the matter is that the first grader indeed does not have the skill set to be able to do long division. What choice does the Stoic have but to accept that? Once he accepts that fact, it no longer offends him. Instead, he can then turn toward being the teacher that moves from someone who expects the person to know long division to someone who can teach that first-grader long division. Which is more practical and productive? This is the second face of forgiveness. It is practicality.

Now let's look at the effectiveness of forgiveness. Forgiveness leads to understanding. When one understands, one is able to forgive; when one forgives, one is able to understand better, and the result snowballs until things get better.

The true Stoic knows that everyone has to learn. Even the Stoic who sits in his chair today is different from the man who sat in his chair yesterday. The last day and the reflection of last night have caused the man to grow, to become wiser, and to see with deeper insight. Could the man of today deem the man of yesterday to be unworthy? Of course not.

If you play that logic out in a thought experiment, you then see that the Stoic who sits in that same chair tomorrow is better than the Stoic who sits there now. Does that mean that the Stoic today is unworthy? If so, he is in the same category of the man who is ignorant. It's problematic because Stoics inherently believe in equity and in equal treatment. If they look pejoratively on the ignorant man, then they would have to do the same to themselves.

Life can't go on that way, and so forgiveness works out to be a better path in harmony and practicality; thus, forgiveness is the imperative that balances the powers of the Stoic. The person who can't forgive the ignorance of another doesn't understand the nature of the world we live in because all things must learn through their mistakes, and sometime the mistakes need to be repeated numerous times before the lesson sticks.

As far as the Stoic is concerned, when he applies forgiveness, he builds empathy, and building empathy deepens the insight of the Stoic. This is the core of study—to be able to forgive us that we can see deeper. Without forgiveness the study is half-baked and thus useless.

However, it is normal to be unable to forgive because of various superseding factors. There is the psychology of the childhood that renders the mind to be unforgiving. There is the mistaken notion that forgiveness promotes complacency, but these notions are not true.

Marcus Aurelius says, "With what are you discontented? With the badness of men? Recall to your mind this conclusion, that rational animals exist for one another, and that to endure is a part of justice, and that men do wrong involuntarily."

Marcus Aurelius was a very forgiving person, but in no way did that translate to be a person who was ineffective. Rome stabilized under his rule.

Wars were won, and peace was ushered in. None of these constituted a small feat or something trivial. He did it by employing Stoic principles, one of which was forgiveness.

Forgiveness is the flavor of study. When we forgive, we are able to open our minds to better understanding. We are able to see the object with better connection in the mind than without forgiveness.

To a certain extent, Stoics are selfish as well as they should be, but their selfish nature is not one of malice. When boarding an aircraft, passengers are instructed that in case of emergencies and when the cabin decompresses to put the oxygen mask on themselves before putting one on their child, even babies. Doesn't this seem selfish? Yes, it does. It is selfish, but in this case that selfishness goes on to be the better action than trying to be selfless and placing the mask on the child first. What happens if the parent passes out? Then who will care for the child?

In the case of the Stoic's selfishness, he is of the mind-set that he needs to perform his industry first so that he can be of greater service to society. We must be able to continue to the world at large, and that is his purpose on earth. His selfish nature, however, does not extend to accumulating rewards and wealth. That is not his interest, and, in fact, to the seasoned Stoic, it can border on being insulting.

Chapter 15 – Discipline

We look at Stoic discipline within the context of invoking concentration and holding it at will, but the power of discipline does extend beyond just this area of need. In the Stoic's life, the discipline that is found at the cerebral level is reflected at the spiritual levels as well. Conversely, the discipline that happens at the cerebral level is also a reflection of the physical aspects of the Stoic. In other words, to have mental discipline, one must have physical discipline.

In cases where it is hard to have mental discipline, turning up the physical discipline makes a credible impact on the mind. There are many ways to invoke physical discipline to be able to enhance the mind. One simple way to do it is to fast or abstain. Fasting and abstinence is a time-honored tradition that has its roots in health and spirituality because it is a powerful tool in building discipline. Just like lifting weights strengthens the biceps, fasting strengthens the resolve, and that strengthens the mind's ability to be disciplined.

Abstinence is a powerful tool. Abstinence can also be related to food, where one reduces consumption of a certain item or reduces the frequency of that item in a period of time. For instance, being vegetarian once a week is a good way to start off showing discipline. Building discipline in one area helps to build it in another area as well. That is the reason why Stoics bring discipline to as many areas of their life as they can so that it keeps their mind and body in check.

Waking up at a time when most people would not consider worth the effort is a strategy the Stoics practice. Not only does it build discipline, but it also clears the mind and makes the inculcation of that discipline easier. Most Stoics arise before the sun, as early as 4 a.m. so that they can phase into the day and find their silence before the day gets busy.

It takes about a week of focused effort to be able make the early rise a habit. Once it builds into a habit, the effort of discipline pays off, and the body starts to appreciate the new discipline that has been instilled.

With early rising and food abstinence and fasting, the major areas of the body's core points of discipline get activated. You can see the effects of those who have the same discipline in getting to the gym every morning before work and those who can control their food intake alter their outward look substantially. But it doesn't stop there. You will notice that these are also the people who go on to succeed in other areas as well because they have learned the key areas of success, which is discipline.

Discipline is the powerful change agent in the body that allows the mind to find ways to realign the neurons that have been developed in a certain pattern. A neurological phenomenon called neuroplasticity allows for the brain to rearrange the patterns that are hard-wired in the brain so that the resulting pattern is different.

The brain also has a safety mechanism. It doesn't allow anyone to randomly and wantonly alter their personality or habit profile, and so it requires sustained effort—not just burst of effort to alter the pattern. Once altered, the new pattern will subsist until another altering event is triggered. This is essentially what discipline is—the ability to expend the necessary effort to make the change that the body already has in place and to do it against the inertia of stability.

Learning discipline in one area allows the mind to realize that it can do it in other areas, and pretty soon the mind is able to do it for all sorts of things. Without discipline the mind tends to fly off the rails, and it begins to do the things that tend to lead to unproductive consequences.

At the same time, too much discipline (yes, there is such a thing) is also not good. Too much discipline alters the happiness in life, and you find yourself in a foul condition at all times. Imagine if you were at the gym nineteen hours a day and slept for the remaining five. It would take tremendous discipline, but it would also alter the happiness quotient in your life. Too much discipline would violate the third part of the foundation—symmetry. Too much of anything causes the symmetry of the whole to tilt out of kilter.

The symmetry of discipline is not indiscipline. You can't be disciplined on one hand and say that you should be undisciplined on the other hand so as to be balanced. It doesn't work that way. The symmetry of discipline is reason.

Reason

To be able to see how reason, discipline, and habit play with each other and how they influence a Stoic, consider the following analogy. Imagine a lazy person who does not like to get up for work. After some time, he gets fired from his job, and he goes out looking for the next job. Luckily, he finds one. Here, too, he doesn't see it fit to wake up on time and keeps getting to the office later. Again, he gets fired. After a few times, he has run out of money and gets kicked out of his apartment. At this point, he realizes the error of his ways and starts to wake up early. He manages to get a job and get back on his feet. He has money for rent, money to eat well, and money to do all the things he wants. He now sees the consequence of getting to work on time.

Now consider a different scenario. A different man can't seem to get himself up to be able to get to work just like the last man. He gets a warning letter from work, and in this scenario, his wife decides that she needs to intervene. She makes it a point to get him to work on time regardless of the difficulty it entails to get him out of bed in the morning. For the next month, she does everything she needs to, and he manages to get to work on time until it is now a habit, and he gets back to being in good graces with the HR department.

In the first scenario, the late riser goes through all the hassle to find the reason that he wants to do things and no longer finds it difficult to do it. In the second scenario, the man goes through a period of altering his mind-set and his waking habit until he is able to alter his waking habits. The first man has found a reason to do what he has to, but the second man didn't find a reason but pushed (or got pushed) into altering his circuits and managed to get out the door without the consequences of pain.

Discipline is like the second scenario except it is an internal matter. The first one is about finding the reason to do something. The first one doesn't need discipline, while the second one does (replace the wife with internal discipline).

There are a few ways to be disciplined. One is to go through the consequences and then reasoning it out so that you don't want to face the consequences, and that naturally motivates the body to do what you need to do. The second is to see the reason and force yourself to do it until the neural pathways in your brain change and you do what needs to be done without any hesitation.

Stoics use both strategies, and they are really good at doing this with reason because they have no time for hyperbole and exaggeration. They know that if X happens, Y will follow. If it rains too heavily, the river will swell. If you drive while inebriated, you are placing yourself and possibly countless other people at risk. Stoics are able to draw a straight line from cause to consequence.

Conclusion

Stoicism is a philosophy that was molded, debated, recast, and presented to the people at large. It was a message that resonated with a large crowd across a wide landscape, from emperor to slave, from Greek to Roman, and from the young to the old. It passed the test of time as it made its way from the lips of Socrates in Athens to the mind of Cato in Rome. Its journey proves that the philosophy, which is really a framework, is one of the most robust of methods to discern the truth and to do it from the mere abilities that we already possess—observe and reflect.

The constant repetition of observation and reflection creates a mental picture of the reality that the Stoic holds true, and eventually it becomes the demeanor in which he operates and the demeanor in which it is recognized for. The man who stands resolute, silent, and strong is often described to be in a Stoic state. The philosophy had entered the mainstream, and it has become an adjective that describes the man of higher intellect and self-control.

The anchoring value of the Stoic is the truth that he seeks and the truth in which he operates. He is concerned with the consequences of poorly conceived actions and the knock-on consequences that would come back to distract him from his path in the future.

The Stoic is not driven by rules and dogma, and he is steadfast but not unreasonable. He is contemplative but not indecisive. He is understanding but not weak. He develops his empathy but stays away from sympathy. The Stoic is a man on a mission, and he knows that the best way to learn about the universe in which he lives is to live the life that he is given. He is not the kind to find a cave and become a hermit. Contemplation indeed has its place, but its place is in the midst of all of life and nature and not hidden in isolation.

Balance is the key to the way of the Stoic. He understands that each path he takes has extremes on either side, and that the balance of those extremes is what makes the world go around. It is not just the balance but the pursuit of the balance that makes life possible. This is the most intimate of Stoic philosophies that needs to be understood at its very core.

Stoicism is not for everybody, although everybody should embrace it so that they can open their eyes. But that would be unrealistic. Since the bottom line of Those who are interested in Stoicism are free to embrace it, but no one should feel pressured. The chances of Stoicism entering the mainstream are slim. On the other hand, there is already a large community that has found the answers that they seem to be in need of, and they have been able to turn their lives around and attach a greater purpose to it. The more people who find their purpose, the better this world would be.

Peace.

If you enjoyed learning about Stoicism, I would be forever grateful if you could leave a review on Amazon. Reviews are the best way to provide feedback to newer authors like myself. It also helps your fellow readers so make sure to help them out! Thanks so much.

Kyle Faber